C000047195

CONFIDENT PARENTING

CONFIDENT PARENTING

A Hands-on Approach to Children

ANNE DAVIS

Drawings by Nicola Wells

SOUVENIR PRESS

To Anne and Luke, Grandma and Grandad, Nannie and Grandad, and Norman and Nicola, without whose support and encouragement this book could never have been written.

Copyright © 1997 by Anne Davis

The right of Anne Davis to be identified as author of this work has been asserted by her in accordance with the Copyright, Designs and Patents Act 1988.

First published 1997 by
Souvenir Press Ltd,
43 Great Russell Street, London WC1B 3PA
and simultaneously in Canada

All Rights Reserved. No part of this publication may be reproduced, stored in a retrieval system or transmitted, in any form or by any means, electronic, mechanical, photocopying, recording or otherwise without the prior permission of the Copyright owner.

ISBN 0 285 63376 7

Typeset by Rowland Phototypesetting Ltd,
Bury St Edmunds, Suffolk

Printed in Great Britain by
Creative Print and Design (Wales), Ebbw Vale

Contents

Acknowledgements 6

PART ONE: THE QUESTION OF DISCIPLINE
1 In the Beginning 9
2 Principles for Parenting 24
3 Grasping the Nettle: To Smack or Not to Smack 41
4 Biting the Bullet: The Truth about Smacking 52

PART TWO: LIVING WITH CHILDREN
5 From Birth to Eighteen Months 79
6 From Eighteen Months to Two and a Half 100
7 From Two and a Half to Three and a Half 121
8 From Three and a Half to Five 142
9 Looking to the Future 165

Notes 171
Index 173

Acknowledgements

Throughout this book I have drawn freely on my own experiences of parenting with my three daughters and have used these to illustrate my points. Elsewhere, when discussing children in general, I have used the masculine pronoun. Likewise, when referring to one parent, I have used 'she' rather than 'he'. No significance should be attached to these gender references which have been adopted for reasons of clarity only. The advice given of course applies equally to either sex.

A.D.

Part One

THE QUESTION OF DISCIPLINE

1 In the Beginning

All of us base our attitudes towards parenting on our own remembered childhood. Our views as adults are coloured by the experience and memory of being parented. If that experience was a happy one, we try to emulate our parents and do as good a job as they did; if our childhood was *not* so happy or downright miserable, we try to ensure that our children will not be able to say the same thing about theirs in twenty years' time. If, as perhaps in most cases, our childhood was basically happy but with a few inconsistencies, we try to ensure that we do not make the same mistakes ourselves. No doubt our own parents made the same resolutions!

For all parents, and for those approaching parenthood, it is fundamentally important and absolutely right that we recognise both the importance of our personal childhood experience and the impact that it has had on the shaping of our adult attitude and approach to children. Especially if there are bad memories, we can learn from them and use them constructively, resolving to work out different and better solutions to the problems that arise. It may be that certain difficulties are avoidable anyway, given the benefit of hindsight and circumstances different from those of our parents. If memories bring back particular injustices or harshness, avoiding the temptation to go to the opposite extreme but, rather, choosing a middle path will almost always be the best approach from our children's point of view. Overcompensating for the failures of our own parents, even with the best motivation, can prove equally extreme and result in a different type of imbalance in a child's experience.

Most adults have a host of memories from their childhood. It's important to use these, especially to reawaken the feelings we experienced as children. They will enable us to identify with our children and help them through certain situations that are common to all generations: for instance, the hurt from feeling left out, lonely or different—for whatever reason—is something most of us can remember experiencing at some point in our childhood. Such remembered emotion may also make us more sensitive to our children's discomfort, embarrassment or frustration. I can remember being intensely irritated as a child when grown-ups said, 'You're too young to understand', when either they couldn't be bothered to explain something or didn't want me to know what they were talking about. I would have preferred the equally honest but gentler, 'Sweetheart, there are some things in life that are very complicated/bad/sad that grown-ups have to try to sort out, but that children don't need to worry about'; or, 'That's a bit difficult to explain right now—let me have a think about it and we'll talk about it later.'

Our remembered feelings can give us great insight into those of our children and, tempered with adult wisdom, can prove invaluable as an aid to understanding them and helping them through the testing times of their childhood.

As parents or future parents we all need something realistic to aim for—perhaps simply to do as well as our parents if we had a happy childhood, or to do better than them if we did not.

Our attitudes towards parenting are also coloured by how we view children *per se*: what is to be their significance in our lives? Are they to fulfil *our* personhood, to be the completion of *our* humanity, giving purpose to *our* lives? Maybe they represent a second chance, a fresh start, new beings into whom frustrated hopes and ambitions can be poured. Perhaps their existence is longed for because of the love, unconditional and free, that they will bring. Or perhaps they will be little accessories to living, reflecting our lifestyle and attitudes, to be proudly displayed like any other cherished possession.

Probably, if we are honest, we will admit that elements of this kind pervade all our thinking—of course we want to be proud of our children, of course we expect them to love us more than anyone else, of course we have great hopes for them, of course they will have a very special place in our lives. But as adults we must not expect or hope to superimpose upon our children *our* personalities, interests or ambitions. Undue emphasis on any one area will, sooner to later, cause disappointment and disruption to the parent–child relationship, and maybe long-term damage in the life of the child. Each baby is a unique and precious individual with inbuilt personality and abilities waiting to unfurl, needing nurture and stimulation, training and encouragement, consistently and lovingly given over many years. Every child will at times be noisy, messy, disobedient, disgusting and downright impossible (possibly all at the same time!); but, equally, each will at times be an absolute joy, and these must sustain us through the bad patches. Parental duty and responsibility include the will to love our children even when we don't like them very much, and the determination not to give up when the going gets tough.

The hopes that we have for our children are clearly linked to the values we hold as adults. Traditionally, many parents have desired that their offspring achieve a 'better' life than themselves, particularly in terms of education, career and financial security. For our children's ultimate happiness, as far as their education is concerned it is important to distinguish between *what* they learn and *why* they learn it. Success, whatever form it takes, should not be simply a means to an end. The child who longs to succeed only because of the positive attention that it will bring is a deprived child indeed. Children of whatever age need approval, affection, time and love, not only as a recompense for their effort, but also to encourage them to keep trying. They need to know that they are loved when they fail. Love should no more be dependent on success than on physical attractiveness.

Too many children are having their values warped by learning that success (coming top, being first, winning games, passing exams) is rewarded by tangible, material gain (money, sweets, gifts), and even that good behaviour and helping around the home may be the subject of bartering. What happens to these children when a reward is not offered, or when they think the promised reward not good enough? Could their conclusion reasonably be that the task is not worth doing? Banal as it may sound, it is nonetheless true that success should be its own reward; goodness and kindness should be acknowledged with thanks and genuine appreciation. Children, like the rest of us, need opportunities to give without demanding, or expecting, something in return and to learn that 'me first' is not a healthy—or happy—attitude to have. They also need to learn that 'playing the game' is fun for its own sake, not only when they win; and that playing by the rules, being honest and fair, is ultimately more satisfying than cheating.

Learning to help, and doing it for its own sake, is an experience that should take place primarily in the home, where such unselfishness and effort can be quietly encouraged, creating an atmosphere where it is welcomed but at the same time accepted as normal. In a home where every little effort or good deed is rewarded with a welter of attention a child may begin to *plan* future 'goodness' in order to trigger the fanfare of praise, rather than be helpful from more genuine motives. This vital approach to life cannot be taught clearly in school where, of necessity, the system teaches that working is indeed about reward—good marks, exam success, achieving the necessary milestones towards a good career, and so on. School is about learning for earning, about making effort that will be recognised. Home is about learning for living, effort being its own reward.

When our children do achieve success, in any of its myriad forms, they sometimes need to be helped towards an appropriate response to that success. Rather than nurturing the feeling that they are superior to their friends and peers, let us as parents encourage the joy of having done well, their satisfaction in having done their best, but also a gladness in having learnt or achieved something new and in being able to understand or do something better today than they could yesterday. Sometimes it may be politic to point out that success is not only about academic, sporting or musical excellence, but that it can also mean being kind, helpful, sensible or *trying* hard; it is not only what we can *do* that can be praiseworthy, but what we *are*.

How children view the challenge of life is largely a measure of their parents' influence and approach: those parents who want their child to be unrestricted and totally uninhibited in their self-expression, to learn exclusively through exploration, may one day wake up to the nightmare of a self-centred child who knows no boundaries, respects no rules, demands constant attention and is probably deeply unhappy, to boot. On the other hand, those parents who give their children freedom within clearly defined limits, who teach them respect and obedience and to value praise that has been earned, not given indiscriminately, will find those children easier to live with, nicer to know, and happier and more secure in their own self-worth. A precocious talent need not belong to a precocious child, but a precocious child will sometimes have little talent other than that for putting other people's backs up.

Parenting has never been a soft option. It has always required sacrifice and self-denial, particularly on the part of the mother, be it through loss of career, of money, of time, of freedom or of energy. Most women would rather bear the challenge of having children, however, than the challenge of not having any.

Parenting also requires a degree of commitment not to be found in any job description on earth—twenty-four hours a day for a minimum of sixteen years, with no paid holidays, sick leave or annual bonus! In our modern era of insular nuclear families and so many broken homes, parenting is an even more daunting task than it was a generation ago. Often the support, trusted advice and back-up from close family simply isn't close enough, geographically or emotionally, and the local community—where such a concept still exists— rarely takes over that role. Neighbours are loath to criticise children for fear of some sort of reprisal, and hesitate to offer advice that might be resented and that would probably, any- way, conflict with modern childcare theory. The siren voices of some childcare gurus wax lyrical on the rights of children, but their words sometimes clash with the underlying ostinato of both common experience and common sense. All this puts more pressure on parents who, although materially better off than *their* parents or grandparents, are often deprived of the practical and emotional support taken for granted by earlier generations.

The challenge for modern parents is to work out their own philosophy of parenting, based on what they want *for* their children and what they expect *from* them. The best starting- point is instinct, backed up by the experience of friends, family *and* the advice of 'experts' *when it does not conflict with personal judgement*. Many childcare professionals are, by the very nature of their work, constantly focusing on children who have been badly or inadequately parented, and what may be appropriate for those children is not necessarily what would be most helpful in a more normal family environment. In any case, 'experts' do not necessarily have the same priorities for children as their parents, and certainly, unless they are counselling them personally, have no knowledge of the indi- vidual child–family relationship.

Probably the most contentious area of modern family life

is that of discipline. Most people agree that it is important but, unlike a generation ago when everyone just got on with it, today there is endless debate and soul-searching as to what is admissible and what is not, what is effective and what is counter-productive, what is good and what is bad. The result of the confusion is often that discipline is approached and applied hesitantly, with lack of conviction. It may be inconsistent or ineffective or even neglected altogether, leaving children with no respect for rules, for possessions or for *other people*. As they grow older they learn that their 'rights' supersede all else, and often acquire an arrogance that is dangerous and yet debilitating. The result of this is seen daily by teachers in many of our schools.

As parents we need to be confident in what we are doing and why—it's not that we should expect to get it right all the time, but at least we should know what we are aiming for. Questions contained in a rhyme quoted to me many years ago in an O-level English class are pertinent here:

> Once I met six wise old men,
> They taught me all I knew.
> Their names were What? and Why? and When?
> And Where? and How? and Who?

What is discipline?

Discipline first of all implies training, aimed at producing obedience and self-control. Second, it implies punishment, given to correct a person or enforce obedience.* The most important aspect of discipline is the former—the teaching, nurturing and encouraging involved in any type of training, but especially the training of young children. If we want our children to be able to fit comfortably and easily into our society we must aim to teach them not only obedience but also a

---

* *The Oxford Dictionary.*

respect for, and understanding of, the rules of the society in which we live. The blind obedience and conformity of soldiers on parade may look impressive, but blind obedience will not teach our children to think for themselves or to develop self-control, or to understand how to behave when the restrictions are removed. Neither will it teach them to appreciate that rules are there for the common good rather than for the purpose of inhibiting personal freedom. Good discipline will help a child conform to what is acceptable without compromising his individuality; it will provide the security and confidence that will enable him to question what he doesn't understand, as well as the consistency necessary for the development of positive, balanced self-esteem.

The punishment aspect of discipline involves taking the most appropriate action, according to the age and understanding of the child, to dissuade him from continuing or repeating the unacceptable behaviour. This could be simply a change in your tone of voice or facial expression, verbal disapproval (a telling-off), a warning of a smack or other penalty such as a period of 'time out' (see page 143), withdrawal of privileges (sweets, pocket money, TV, treats), or the imposition of some task to 'undo' the problem caused by the naughtiness or disobedience.

Why is discipline necessary?

We all need to encourage our children to be good—kind, obedient, respectful; but they manage to be naughty—rude, defiant, selfish—without any prompting from us! They cannot learn to behave in a socially acceptable way, to distinguish right behaviour from wrong behaviour, unless they are *taught* to do so—by example as well as by instruction. A child who was never spoken to would not develop speech; he would be condemned to making inarticulate noises in order to express his needs and frustrations. Even if he were given extensive speech therapy as a young adult, he would never fully recover anything like full powers of speech or expression. And the same is true of learning right from wrong. The child who has not been taught right from wrong, good from bad, in those pre-school years, who has not learned to respect people or rules, will find it very difficult to acquire those values in school—no matter how dedicated his teachers. We teach and discipline our children because it is our parental responsibility to do so, for their sake, for our sake and for that of the wider community. Moreover, we do so because we want our children to grow from happy, secure, well adjusted little people into fulfilled, balanced and confident 'big people'. This is the aim: that our children shall fit easily into nursery or school, and from then on into all the other social groupings that they will encounter in their ever-expanding world.

When should we discipline?

The training aspect of discipline should be a gentle conditioning, beginning almost from birth. In practice this means that we as parents add a discipline, or routine, to things we have not had to think about before—simple things, such as giving baby a bath before bedtime (providing a recognisable and relaxing precursor to sleep), and not switching on the light when feeding him during the night (so as not to wake him up any more than is necessary). Of course, tiny babies cannot be 'naughty' any more than they can be 'good'; they can be happy (content) or unhappy, comfortable or uncomfortable, awake or asleep, but not a great deal more than that. As a baby grows he will begin to develop interests and preferences, but it is not until he begins to be mobile that he can make active choices about some of his actions—and that's when the fun really starts!

When children have *chosen* to be naughty, it is almost always appropriate for some sort of penalty to be incurred, to act not purely as punishment but also as a deterrent to repeating the 'bad' behaviour. With very young children it is crucial that any such correction be given immediately, in order for them to connect it with their misdeed. In many cases verbal displeasure will be enough; little children do not like their parents being cross with them, unless it is the only way they can get their attention. 'Wait until your father gets home' is not an appropriate response here, and would be both confusing and damaging to a child's understanding of right and wrong and also to his relationship with his father.

As children reach school age it may become appropriate to apply certain 'delayed' punishments (such as cancelling next week's pocket money, imposing an early bedtime, banning a favourite TV programme), but it is pointless to do so unless the child fully understands why such action is being taken. It is equally pointless to promise it but not follow it through.

As a general rule, with children up to the age of five penalties for bad behaviour should be applied immediately, not left hanging in the balance. No one likes to have a dark cloud hovering over them, and such a policy avoids the danger of resentment building up over the delayed retribution as well as sidestepping the potential problem of more bad behaviour that such resentment could set off. 'Instant justice' also avoids the confusion created in a small child when he is punished for an earlier misdemeanour that he has long since put behind him and forgotten about. And it confounds the inescapable logic in the mind of the child that delayed punishment actually means *double* punishment: the initial telling-off and then the later penalty.

Where should we discipline?

The best place to discipline a child is usually as close as possible to the scene of the crime! If he has knocked something over, get him to clear up the mess (or at least get him to help you to do it). If he has done something requiring a telling-off or a smack, do it straight away and *on the spot*, unless there are other children present who would enjoy the spectacle or in front of whom the child would show off. In such a case either banish the would-be spectators to another room, or take the guilty party to one. However, contrary to popular modern theory, a little bit of embarrassment will cause no lasting psychological hang-up in the child, but could in fact have a salutary effect. (Many believe, indeed, that with some adult offences the threat of public exposure and the ensuing humiliation would be a far more effective deterrent than a fine or community service. Shame, including the risk of bringing shame on those we love, is an important factor that could be used to powerful and positive effect by a judiciary with the courage and wisdom to apply it. For our children we are both judge and jury, and there are times when we too need courage and wisdom in dealing justly with them.)

If you think that a smack is the most suitable method of dealing with a situation, give it in a disciplined way—not a frantic swipe—on the child's hand or leg.

How should we discipline?

How we discipline our children, whether from the training or the deterrent angle, depends largely on two factors: our motivation and our own self-control. If our motivation for wanting well disciplined children is based on the desire for an ordered life, with children trained to 'perform' —look good, be good/clever/talented/funny—when required but ready to slip uncomplainingly into the background when not, then we need to reassess our appraisal of our children as individuals, admitting their need to be wanted and loved *for their own sake* as opposed to being a means of satisfying our pride or ambition. If our motivation is centred on our children's needs, it will take into account their emotional as well as their physical and cognitive development.

When our first child reaches toddling stage, self-control as parents is something many of us discover we are strangely lacking. (Some of us will have found out even before that!) We have to learn to cope not only with his tiny tantrums but with our own frustrated temper as well. Self-discipline is something most of us need to work at, not least because it is hard work being consistently equable, patient, steadfast, loving and *there*! The fact that we are not always the epitome of these qualities is not cause for despondency, but confirms that we are only human and, like our children, need to keep on trying.

As already noted, the practical application of discipline as a punishment or deterrent should vary according to the age, understanding and experience of the child. Each situation is different, and it would be foolish to prescribe a set course of action without knowledge and understanding of both child and circumstance.

Who should discipline?

Parents must bear the primary responsibility for discipline. In order to fulfil our basic task of bringing up our children in such a way as to enable them one day to fit in and contribute positively to adult society, we must set limits for their behaviour and reinforce those limits when they are challenged. Parents can ask other adults whom they trust and who are closest to their children—grandparents, neighbours, childminders, close friends—to share this responsibility. Hopefully, these will be people who not only *spend* time with the children but also *give* them time. Young children will always respond more positively to discipline imposed by adults they love and want to please, and will try harder to gain their approval and praise. Attempts by people they do not know or trust or like to enforce any aspect of discipline will probably be met with resentment, tears or confusion, and are best avoided.

As children get older, they will come under the discipline of their teachers. But if the basic groundwork of respect and obedience has not been established in the pre-school years there is little that any teacher can do to make up that deficit— unless with the full, if belated, cooperation of the parents.

Bringing up children is hard work, but it isn't *all* hard work. Laughter and fun, kisses and cuddles are a hugely important part of family life, however old or young the child. As flowers need the sun, so babies, little children and bigger children too need loving physical contact with those closest to them. Loving our children *and letting them know that we love them* is the most important thing that any parent can do. The security of a cuddle is more precious than words can say, whether to a toddler or to a gangly eleven-year-old. And it's worth remembering that affection isn't shown only through hugs, but also through horseplay! Most children enjoy being chased by a trusted adult or wrestling on the floor, or being thrown up and caught again (when they're little and light enough!), or being swung round in the garden or park. Quieter forms of physical affection, such as holding hands on the way to school, are simple and almost unconscious ways of showing that we care.

However, children cannot always have our full and instant attention the moment they want it. Here touch has an important role to play, in helping them learn to wait. Any mother of pre-school children will confirm that they will inevitably 'need' her the minute she's on the phone—especially if it's an important call! Hissing 'Shhhhhh' through clenched teeth or muttering 'I won't be a minute' rarely has any effect on a three-year-old who wants to show you his Duplo aeroplane

Any mother of pre-school children will confirm that her children will inevitably 'need' her the minute she's on the phone.

now, or on a five-year-old wanting to know the contents of tomorrow's lunch box, or even a seven-year-old who's lost one of her school plimsolls! But a hand resting on their head or shoulder will make their waiting easier, because they understand that they have at least part of your attention and that they will be your first priority when the phone call is finished.

The importance of touch in the lives of our children cannot be overstated. The quiet cuddle, the unrestrained romp, the admonishing hand, the consoling hug, the kissing better of hurts (real or imagined)—all have their place at different stages.

Of course, as already mentioned, nobody should expect to get it right all the time, but hindsight combined with experience is a great teacher for those who are willing to learn. Remember that although we may wish to be the perfect mother or father, our children don't want or need perfect parents—and what an impossible example to live up to that would be, anyway! Much better to have an imperfect but loving parent who can admit getting it wrong and even says sorry sometimes.

The key to good discipline is the combination of love for the child and self-control on the part of the parent, juxtaposed with reasonable expectations for the behaviour of both. Children learn as much by observation as by tutelage; the example of their parents' behaviour and attitudes will have a more powerful influence on them than those of any other human being, and will serve to bless or blight the rest of their lives. This is the awful significance of parenting, and the awesome responsibility of parenthood.

2 Principles for Parenting

It is in the family that we learn the importance of mutual respect and that self-respect must be developed by a respect for others.

—Tony Blair

PRINCIPLE a basic truth or general law or doctrine that is used as a basis of reasoning or a guide to action or behaviour.

—Oxford Dictionary

There are two types of principle involved in raising children: principles for us and principles for them! Principles for parents to remember include the following:

- Children respond better to demonstrative love, interest and praise than to understated love, indifference or criticism.
- Our children need consistency and confidence from us, not uncertainty, frequent negotiation or constant compromise. (Compromise has its place, but should not be habitually expected, like bargaining in a Turkish bazaar.)
- We should expect obedience from our children. If we *don't* expect it, our expectations will be exhaustingly fulfilled!
- Children assimilate attitudes and learn responses through *their experience of our example.*
- Bad behaviour may be the symptom rather than the cause of a problem.
- Children will only push us over the edge if we haven't shown them clearly where it is.
- No normal child under the age of seven understands the course of action required of him on hearing the request,

'Hurry up' (especially first thing in the morning). Flogging a dead horse comes to mind here.

- Little children *can* be both reasonable and rational (especially when they are asleep). At all other times, prepare for logic to be discarded with the first stamp of a tiny foot.

There are only two principles for our children to learn, but they encompass all that is relevant to properly equip young minds and emotions to face the adventure of life:

- Each child needs to absorb the reality that he is loved *unconditionally*; that he is valued *for himself*, not for what he can do.
- Each child needs to be taught the difference between right and wrong and *encouraged always to choose what is right*. This should include the distinction between things that are wrong and wrong ways of doing things.

The knowledge that he matters—that he is wanted, loved and appreciated—is fundamentally important to the emotional well-being of every child. It not only provides a crucial sense of security (the basis of a healthy self-image), but also creates the starting-block for an appreciation that *other people matter too*. The child who is talked to and played with, and who learns that his words and actions have consequences—and that the most rewarding consequences come when he is good— will be secure and happy within the known limits of his world. A growing appreciation that, just as other people do things to make him happy, so he also can behave in a way to make *them* happy, marks the beginning of his perception that other people's feelings matter. Knowing how to please, wanting to please and having the opportunity to do so are all essential for the development of a healthy self-image and for a sound appreciation of the value of others.

The child who is used to being rubbished, laughed at or ignored, who constantly hears negative instruction ('Stop it!',

'Shut up!', 'Leave it alone!', 'Don't touch!'), who is left with the TV for company, will feel that he has no value and no importance in the life of his family. Consequently, he will believe that he really *doesn't* matter. If he doesn't matter, it doesn't matter what he does, because no one is really interested. And if no one cares about him, why should he care about anyone else? Such a child, unused to speaking up for himself or to being listened to, is likely either to become a victim of bullying at some stage in his school career or to become a bully himself, as a means of experiencing some power, prestige or recognition for himself. His own negative self-image and lack of a feeling of self-worth will warp his perception of the world around him, and unless something happens to break the cycle will turn him from a rejected, unhappy child into a rejected, unbalanced adult.

Right and wrong, 'naughty' and 'No!'

Teaching the difference between right and wrong begins the first time we say 'no' to a baby. Tiny children have no innate understanding of what is right and wrong—they have to be taught it. Many babies and toddlers have a fascination with hair (other people's) and love to pull it—especially when they get a big reaction! They need to be dissuaded from doing so as quickly as possible by firm use of the word 'No' and equally firm use of restraint—disengaging their sticky fingers from the object of their desire, and then keeping them at a safe distance while if possible providing something equally engaging for them to fiddle with.

The task of teaching right from wrong, good from bad, safe from dangerous, is not completed until the child himself is independently able to discern the difference in any given situation. The parental responsibility then shifts from what may have been an authoritarian and dogmatic position to a supportive back-up role, encouraging the child to use his knowledge wisely—maybe courageously—and *choose* what is right or good or best. Knowing what is right is less than half the battle, of course: the real challenge is in doing it, even (and especially) when that means being different and standing out against the crowd. Being willing to choose what is right for its own sake— understanding that honesty and truth matter—marks the development of conscience.

'No' is a hugely important word for little children to hear, but only if they are trained to respond to it positively, and if it is counterbalanced with appropriate use of 'Yes'. The only way they can learn that some activities are unacceptable is by doing them, or attempting to do them, and perceiving from our response that it would be better not to repeat that particular exploration or experiment. When they do try to repeat the behaviour, they are testing to see if it is still a no-no. It is important that we do not confuse the issue for them by changing the rules, or by sometimes letting them get away with it merely because we are tired, in a hurry or have friends round. Children gain great security from knowing the rules, and confidence from the knowledge that those rules will not change. This does not mean that they won't try to get round them, but it will help them accept that 'it's a fair cop' when they're caught!

There is a notion currently gaining ground that it is so overridingly important to encourage and be positive towards our children that they should never experience negatives—not so much 'Never say never' as 'Never say no'. The philosophy behind this is that to say no to a child is to inhibit his self-expression, thus restricting his freedom; that it is an assault on his right to make his own choices and so prevents him from learning from experience. For the sake of sanity, and for the sake of our children, let's hope that most parents are guilty as charged. Being positive is one thing, but promoting positives to the exclusion of all negatives is quite something else and would foster an imbalance in the child's perception of the world.

Shortly after my High Court victory in 1994, I met an experienced and competent childminder from Merton in south-west London. She had been told by her social worker that there was no such thing as 'naughty children', just naughty behaviour. Consequently, according to the social worker, she should no longer employ 'the naughty chair'—a form of 'time out' (see page 143)—to discipline her charges, and she should delete the word 'naughty' from her vocabulary when talking to them. When the childminder asked what would happen should she refuse to comply, she was told that she would be deregistered by the Local Authority (and therefore unable legally to childmind. All childminders have to be registered by their Local Authorities). 'OK then, sack me,' said the child-minder. The social worker, clearly flustered, took her leave, and nothing more was said of the matter. This particular child-minder was a university graduate who had taken time out to look after her children; sadly, not all childminders, in the face of the all-powerful social services, have her confidence and self-assurance.

Who knows how many others have been threatened into accepting contentious, if not nonsensical, dogma or forced to compromise on what they perceive to be the truth of a situation? Also in 1994, a bemused postgraduate student reported that at the nursery school in London where she was on teaching practice, the head teacher had forbidden the staff to say no to the children. In 1995 the assistant secretary to the National Association of Head Teachers commented: 'For many pupils the first time they hear the word "No" is when they start school.' Some children do not even hear it there.

While it is foolish to label a child as 'naughty' or 'stupid' or 'greedy'—any child will resent such condemnation and, furthermore, will be likely to believe the label and live up to it if he hears it too often—it is nevertheless a nonsense to throw out the concept of naughtiness. Naughty things don't just happen: they are not acts of nature (those are accidents!), but the result of a conscious decision on the part of the child to do something he knows he should not. To ignore such behaviour, or to merely distract a child from it, gives the message that it doesn't *really* matter. Not punishing bad behaviour is a sure way of seeing it repeated; not acknowledging it is to head for certain disaster. Children need to hear the word 'No'—and they need to hear it *as soon as they begin to misbehave*, before they really begin to enjoy themselves! Putting an early and unmistakable stop to potentially bad behaviour will dampen not the child but only the naughtiness, and will militate against more aversive sanctions later. Besides, children need strong leadership; they respond well to clearly defined rules, they respect firm management and gain a sense of security from it through the belief that Mummy (or Daddy, or teacher) not only knows best but also wants what is best for them.

In fact, 'No' is a positive word! It provokes a change of action, attitude or understanding and is essential to the experience of every small child. It is also an absolute, which children can respect even if they don't like or understand it ('No, you may not have another helping of ice-cream/watch that film/ wear your wellies in bed'). Where appropriate it can be softened with 'because . . .' or an alternative suggestion ('No, you can't do that, but you can try this', 'No, not now—maybe tomorrow'). And sometimes it can stand its ground, backed up by 'Because I said so' in the tone of voice that brooks no opposition. Children need to understand that not all adult decisions are negotiable or under constant review; they need to experience that 'No' can be both final and absolute, and learn to respect it even—especially—when they don't, or can't, understand it. (Bedtime in summer, for instance, is a constant battle zone for many parents 'because it isn't dark yet'.) A child who is trained to respond obediently to 'No'

Children need to hear the word 'No' ... before they really begin to enjoy themselves.

is one who can be confident in his parents' judgement and authority.

We should never be embarrassed or ashamed to say no to our children if we do so because we have their best interests at heart. The flip side of teaching the morality of 'No' when children are small is that it may help them to say no to things they know to be wrong when they are older, rather than be swept along with the crowd.

Psychological principles in the socialisation of children

Some children are harder to socialise than others
Any parent of more than one child will confirm that each has a distinct character, significantly different from his siblings', and that each may react in a totally different way to the same stimulus or circumstance.

Some mothers suspect a different personality type from the

moment of birth, and often later find their assessment to have been remarkably accurate. My daughters are a case in point. The first arrived apparently angry and yelling at the world, and continued to be a hard-to-please and very determined little character who wanted to do everything herself without assistance or instruction. Her sometimes destructive desire to achieve has matured into an appreciation of what she wants, and a determination to work for it and to enjoy the recognition and praise that it will bring. My second daughter arrived calm, undemanding and utterly laid-back. She continued to be an 'easy' baby, generally happy without ever demanding a great deal of attention. She was more self-sufficient in that she would play imaginatively, alone, quite happily and for much longer than her older sister; but, faced with concrete tasks with set objectives (puzzles, colouring and so on), she would flit from one to the other with no sustained interest in anything that required real effort. Confronted with the inevitability of school and the discipline of having to finish certain tasks in order to change activity, after a brief rebellion she nevertheless conformed to what was expected of her. But she still only applies herself wholeheartedly when she is interested in the activity rather than on account of any praise that such application may bring her. My third baby had to be strongly induced to leave the womb at all, and throughout her first two years was unmistakably less secure, more clinging and more of a 'mummy's baby' than either of her sisters had been.

Psychologists agree that children are born with individual sets of characteristics, that they inherit certain features of personality in the same way that they inherit other characteristics such as eye and hair colour, height and build, intelligence, sporting and artistic ability. One psychologist has commented, in an article on the psychology of smacking children, 'It has now been established beyond any doubt that genetic endowment determines very marked differences in temperament.'[1] What this means is that some babies are easier to socialise (civilise!) than others. The child who is polite, respectful, good, kind and obedient may be so not solely thanks to the parenting skills of his mother and father, but also because he has a passive, eager-to-please personality. Conversely, some children are more difficult to bring up, requiring much more effort, imagination and dedication (or blood, sweat and tears) on the part of their parents. According to the American psychologist David T. Lykken, 'there are certain innate characteristics that make some children harder than others to socialize. As a rule, children who are more venturesome, impulsive or aggressive, less intelligent or less talented, are harder to socialize successfully.'[2] As that must embrace at least half the children who ever draw breath, it is reassuring to learn from the same source that 'the principles involved in the successful socialization of "difficult" children are the ones that also work the best with children of average temperament'. Lykken agrees that the basic ground rule for the successful socialisation of any child is the early establishment of a loving relationship with his parents; upon this foundation all future successful teaching, training and nurture depend.

Boys and girls—Vive la différence!

As a mother of girls, I am loath to admit that girls are actually easier to socialise than boys, particularly since during her first three years my first-born would have been described as 'a typical boy' had she happened to have been born male! However, there is significant research evidence to suggest that many boys *are* harder to socialise than their sisters. This is reflected in the obvious difference in the ratio of male prisoners to female ones, and in the experience of many primary teachers that the most unruly children are more often boys than girls.

Research in the United States reveals that the lifetime prevalence of antisocial personality disorder in that country is 7.3 per cent in men and 1 per cent in women.[3] But as a non-psychologist I wonder how many of those antisocial personalities—and, equally, how many disruptive boys in school—are that way not because they are innately more difficult to socialise but because they have had no consistent, positive male role-model on whom to base their behaviour and attitudes during their formative years. While I wholeheartedly endorse the sentiment that 'families need fathers', it seems to me even more inescapable that boys in particular need their dads—or, at the very least, another close male figure who takes an interest in them and to whom they can relate.

One controversial but highly revealing experiment in the USA studied the effect of long-term committed male volunteer 'mentors' on boys in a class of underprivileged children in a city 'sink' school. The volunteers came into school weekly to each help one boy, building a relationship with that particular child and encouraging him to develop positive aspirations rather than acquiesce to the underclass culture of many of the men with whom he came into daily contact. The results of the study showed that over the years the delinquent tendencies of this group were greatly reduced in comparison with a similar control group without the mentor scheme.

Men have a huge responsibility to be committed to their children, and especially to their sons; fathers and mothers have a huge responsibility to be committed to each other as well as to their children.

The parental role

A fundamental law of psychology states that behaviour that is followed by a satisfying state of affairs is strengthened, and behaviour followed by a dissatisfying state of affairs is weakened.[4] The emphasis here is on balance: punishment and criticism of bad behaviour must be balanced by praise and encouragement of good behaviour.

Lykken has stated: 'Socialization is the product of two factors: *parenting* and *innate characteristics*.'[5] This seems to me a commonsense acknowledgement that the children we produce are the result of both nurture and nature: as parents we have to build positively on whatever raw material comes with the squirming little bundle the midwife places in our arms. A recognition of the significance of 'nurture' also confers a social responsibility to offer guidance and practical help to parents who are struggling with this side of the equation, and to recognise the hopeless downward spiral that can result when such help is not available.

In any discussion of the discipline or socialisation of children it is recognised that the most fundamental factor is the relationship between the parent and the child. Well socialised parents, who are most likely to pass on their values and produce well socialised children, are those who not only have a loving and secure relationship with their children but who confidently, consistently and caringly teach them right from wrong from the very earliest age; and who proceed to build on their relationship by spending time with them and by being aware of and influencing their activities when they are apart. Conversely, psychologists in the United States reported in 1989 that 'families of antisocial children are characterized by harsh and inconsistent discipline, little positive parental involvement with the child, and poor monitoring and supervision of the child's activities'.[6]

Socialisation is learnt primarily from parents. It is both irresponsible and unrealistic for parents to attempt to delegate that duty to the school; when a child reaches school age, the mould for his behaviour and attitudes has already been set. Breaking that mould and creating a new one—if it is thought advisable to try to do so—is no casual affair: it is a full-time labour of love that few other than full-time, committed parents are qualified to undertake.

In British law parental responsibility includes the right of reasonable chastisement.

The law

Under British statute and in common law parents have responsibility for their children, and this includes the 'right of reasonable chastisement'. Parents also have the right to delegate this latter responsibility to someone they have chosen to care for their child. This could be a nanny or childminder, or staff at an independent school where corporal punishment is still used.

Article 19 of the UN Convention on the Rights of the Child requires signatories to 'take all appropriate legislative, administrative, social and educational measures to protect the child from all forms of physical or mental violence, injury or abuse, neglect or negligent treatment, maltreatment or exploitation, including sexual abuse, while in the care of parent(s), legal guardian(s) or any other person who has care of the child.' The British government's view has consistently been that smacking should not be included in the definition of abuse; it has always maintained that Article 19 should be read in conjunction with Article 5, which obliges states to respect a parent's responsibilities to provide appropriate direction and guidance for her child, thus indirectly affirming that the best place for a child to grow up is in the family and that primary responsibility for the authority over the child rests with the parents, not with the state.

The British government ratified the UN Convention in December 1991, and it was not until later that the UN Commissioners reached a definitive explanation of Article 19, bringing ordinary smacking into the 'abuse' category and adopting the position favouring the prohibition of all forms of corporal punishment.

Common sense

As adults we obey laws and rules for one of two reasons. Either we agree with the basic validity and good sense of a given rule and are happy to comply with it, or we acquiesce because we are aware of—and fear—the consequences of breaking it. Sometimes we may take our chances and flout a particular restriction, but we know that we may have to pay the penalty for doing so—quite literally, where traffic wardens are involved!

Generally, children are no different from adults in this respect. However, the very young do not yet have the ability to agree or disagree with the sense of any rule. They have neither the experience nor the understanding that leads to acceptance and compliance, and so it is of paramount importance to make any penalties appropriate and relevant. A baby cannot understand why people make such interesting faces when their hair is pulled; a two-year-old has no conception of the potential danger that an unknown dog may bring with it, particularly if his only experience of dogs is of his own friendly pet; a three-year-old can have no grasp of the problems he could cause by 'playing' with the telephone; a four-year-old may have great difficulty with the idea that he needs to eat carrots and greens when he would much prefer chocolate and cake.

All of these everyday situations call for an appropriate response that will dissuade the child from repeating that particular approach to, or exploration of, his world. Initially this may have to be a negative response—a firm 'No', a restraining hand, a verbal warning, a pudding forfeited! For some children, in some circumstances, a smack may be needed as back-up to the instruction or reasoning that has already been offered. But once children understand the boundaries for their behaviour they usually stay within them, even when they can't appreciate the reasoning that necessitates them. Part of the concept of respect for parental authority, continually growing within the child, is an acceptance that Mummy (or Daddy) knows best, even though this sometimes conflicts with the child's desires. Of course, children, like their parents, are sometimes inclined to try their luck or risk an occasional sortie into forbidden territory—perhaps on the off chance that they won't be found out or because the lure of the temptation is greater than any concern they might feel about the known penalty. Sometimes penalties have to be reassessed and possibly changed, in order to get across the message that disobedience costs more than it pays. More often it is simply a question of making sure that the penalties remain consistent.

Children, like adults, will disregard a rule:

- if they do not fear or do not dislike the consequence of breaking it. This strongly suggests that the consequence is ineffectual because it is inappropriate.

- if they do not believe that the consequence will be applied—in which case it is no deterrent. 'Do that again and I'll kill you!' is a classic.
- if they do not believe that they will be caught or found out. Part of responsible parenting is an awareness of the need to be vigilant; to monitor our children's activities.
- if it appears to be arbitrary. Rebuking a child one day but ignoring similar behaviour the next is confusing for the child and not conducive to respect for the parent. Lack of consistency in one area can undermine parental authority in others.
- if they do not understand what is expected of them. When reasoning with very little children it is important to speak clearly, and it can also help to speak slowly. Physical proximity is important; instruction from across the room is likely to be less effective than a few carefully chosen words on or by mother's knee. Holding a child's hands, or putting an arm around him while you talk, helps his concentration; eye contact will help you to 'read' his understanding—or lack of it—from his face.

While it is important to establish understood boundaries for behaviour, it is also important to recognise that the penalty for pushing at or breaking those boundaries need not be the same for each child. Clearly, one would not apply the same consequence to a four-year-old scribbling over a book as to a one-year-old, but two children of a similar age committing the same 'crime' may also receive different penalties—providing they have not been conspirators in their mischief-making! It may be an effective deterrent for one child to be smacked for scribbling over a book, but it may be more effective for another to 'lose' his pencils for a day or two, or perhaps be restricted to a lead pencil for a time. A more constructive punishment might involve the *proper use* of pencils—for instance, the careful colouring of a picture, requiring much concentration and what for the child may constitute considerable effort and hard work.

Children have to learn what is unacceptable—dangerous, naughty, irritating, nasty, selfish, rude—through the socialisation process that is childhood. But obedience is not only about restricting or restraining unwanted behaviours; it is also about maximising good times and good habits. The child who is obedient will have more time to enjoy his activities than one who wastes time arguing, procrastinating and being defiant. Also, he will have parents with more energy and enthusiasm than the child who is allowed to drive his to exhaustion.

Giving time to children does not mean, for example, *discussing* at length with a three-year-old why he should wear a coat in the middle of January: tell him that he has to wear the coat *and why*, but debating the issue should not come into the scheme of things—delayed obedience is simply disobedience in a more subtle form.

Sometimes defiance in small things can lead to a child missing out on big pleasures; sometimes it can lead to other children missing out as well. Visiting the coast with friends one winter, one child in the group refused to wear wellies, despite having it explained to him that salt water and shoe leather do not mix and despite the fact that everyone else (including the adults) was clad in rubber from the knees down. Arriving at the beach, all the children rushed down to paddle, including the wellyless one who was wearing his new leather school shoes. He did not appreciate being hauled out of the waves, and proceeded to sulk at being singled out from the others. Not splashing and chasing around with the rest, he quickly became cold, with the result that we all had to return to base early, thus cutting short the fun of the other four children. Because of the defiance of one child, all suffered. Such situations are for adults to learn from as well as children—the next time we visited the beach, despite initial reluctance everyone wore their welly-boots, and a great time was had by all.

One of the most important principles in parenting is the appropriate use of the word 'sorry' when *we* get things wrong. Parents are people, too, and make mistakes just like anyone else. Saying sorry to our children will not diminish us in their eyes: it will reassure them after what may have seemed an unfair or 'over the top' reaction from us. It provides the best possible example for them to follow, and their ready forgiveness will be a potent lesson for us. It may also help reassure guilt-stricken parents that they aren't hopeless failures after all, and that their children still love them, warts and all! Forgiveness can only be activated through genuine use of the confession, 'I'm sorry', but it is a powerful ally indeed to have on your side.

3   Grasping the Nettle: To Smack or Not to Smack

. . . in certain circumstances it may be necessary and sensible to administer a smack to your child.

—*HRH Prince Charles*

There has been a great deal of debate in recent years over the rights and wrongs of smacking, be it in the home or at school—and, more recently, over whether it should be done by parents or by other adults. The debate will not go away, of course; even in Sweden, which has had a smacking ban since 1979, there has been recent discussion in the media about the wisdom of the anti-smacking legislation. The debate centres on two opposing camps: one believes that they know best how to discipline their own children, and the other believes that they know how best to discipline everyone else's children as well and would impose that belief by law, given half a chance. Such is the divide between the vast majority of ordinary parents and the tiny but vociferous army representing, in the main, the Children's Rights movement. To claim, as they do, that a smack is likely to lead to physical abuse is akin to saying that a cuddle is likely to lead to sexual abuse. To state that banning smacking will eradicate physical abuse is not only provocative, but surreal. One is tempted to wonder if the bottom line in all this might not be that there is rather more money—and reputations—to be made from the Children's Rights industry than from promoting parental responsibilities. Indeed, a recent call for a 'Children's Rights Commissioner' suggested that such a post would require a staff of fifty, and a budget of four *million* pounds.[1]

The reality is that most parents do smack—even in Sweden. A recent survey revealed that 50 per cent of parents there admitted to smacking their children, despite it being an illegal act.[2] We have no reason to believe that most of those children won't grow up to become loving, responsible parents who in their turn will also occasionally smack their children. Of course the reality, that most parents do smack their children, should no more be taken to mean that smacking is *always* the answer to bad behaviour than that it is *always* wrong. Any parent who consistently smacks her child through lack of patience or loss of temper will damage that child, psychologically if not physically. A parent who constantly shouts at and denigrates her child or who ignores him will achieve the same sad result. This much is common sense—we do not need childcare 'experts' to tell us so. When their pronouncements confirm the reality of our experience they can generally be regarded as an accurate reflection of life; but when they negate or deny that reality their statements must be viewed with a healthy scepticism and tirelessly probed with common sense.

When is it right to smack?

If a child has been deliberately and repeatedly defiant, a smack is the unmistakable and immediate signal, to him, that he has gone too far. It will also serve as a deterrent as far as that particular behaviour is concerned, and remind him that the balance of power between parent and child is not an equal one. Children do not have equal rights with their parents, any more than they have equal responsibilities with them. They do not possess the emotional or mental maturity, or the experience, or the *will* to cope with such rights. Of course, our children do have a great many rights, but very different ones from those that we claim as adults, and substantively different,

I suggest, from many claimed for them by the Children's Rights movement.

The other instance when a smack is appropriate is when one child has deliberately hurt another. First, it teaches the aggressor not only that he won't get away with such behaviour, but also that pain is an unpleasant experience and best avoided whenever possible. Second, it demonstrates to the victim that his hurt matters—that *he* matters—and that his aggressor has been justly dealt with. It also helps to eliminate the natural desire of the hurt child to get his own back, and to remove the fear of the offence being repeated. Young children have a very keen sense of fairness, and it is important in their eyes that justice be *seen* to be done; simply telling off or reasoning with the aggressor will do little to salve the sense of indignity or fear of reprisal left hanging in the mind of the victim.

Children are sometimes smacked in a less controlled manner—for instance, by a parent who, traumatised and trembling, has just watched helplessly as her child has run into the road. This scenario does not fall into either of the first two categories, but the terror and relief embodied in that smack will serve to forcibly impress upon the child that he must never, ever, do it again. And contrary to the claims of some psychologists, most children will remember not only the wallop, but also the reason for it.

When is it wrong to smack?

More often than not, is the short answer! As parents we need to develop the ability to analyse quickly our children's 'naughtiness' and to recognise that, far from being deliberate, what appears to be bad behaviour or disobedience may be the symptom, not the cause, of a problem. Often it may simply be the best way for a child to be sure of getting our attention. In our busy, clock-centred lives we play and talk with our children when *we* make the time, but this does not necessarily fit in with when *they* want a cuddle or a chat. Naughtiness may be the result of a child feeling that any attention is better than none, or even of a 'tit for tat' notion whereby he rationalises his bad behaviour on the grounds of his parents' perceived rejection. It may be highly inconvenient to set aside the spud-bashing, hoovering, letter-writing or whatever in order to have a quick cuddle with your two-year-old, or a short dance with your three-year-old or a Chinese lantern demo with your four-year-old, but it can be more constructive to give him a few minutes' positive, willing, full-time attention before continuing with the task than to ignore him and have to deal with the ensuing mess or bad temper afterwards.

A smack should not be a mechanism for relieving adult anger. It is not necessarily wrong to smack *when* we are angry, but it is always wrong to smack *because* we are angry. Smacking is justified on the grounds of a child's behaviour, not of an adult's feelings. The motivation for smacking should be for the good of the child, not the expurgation of the parent. There is a very real danger that if we smack because we are angry we will actually release that anger on to our precious child who, instead of a disciplinary smack, will suffer an undisciplined thrashing. At best, this will fill us with guilt and remorse; at worst, we could seriously hurt our child.

If a child has already worked himself into a tantrum, a smack *may* shock him out of it, but it is more likely to prolong it. The best policy in such cases is usually to leave well alone until he has exhausted himself, and then gently gather up the pieces. If the child is very young, it may be appropriate to put him in his cot until he has calmed down; if he is older, the bedroom will suffice. If the outburst is likely to last only a few minutes (judging from previous occasions), leave him where he is, but don't look on anxiously waiting for it to pass—any type of audience, no matter how sympathetic, will only serve to prolong the performance. The quickest way to calm a tantrum is to ignore it. When it is over the child will usually want a reassuring cuddle; this may be a good time to talk, explaining why you wouldn't acquiesce to his demands and perhaps suggesting an alternative course of action for him, should the situation recur. The calm after the storm can often be a time of great value for both parent and child, when the heaving sobs of temper are transformed into the healing tears of penitence.

Common causes of frustration for adults which are *not* resolved by smacking include a universal ability on the part of children to forget almost everything important that we ever tell them (they have different priorities); the medical condition known as 'selective deafness' (inherited from their fathers, as most mothers will confirm); an uncanny capacity to misunderstand the adult viewpoint; a clumsiness out of all proportion to their size, and a magnetic attraction to all things dirty, wet and generally undesirable.

How should we smack?

Used wisely, a smack can be the most effective method of correcting defiant or aggressive behaviour. Deliberate, repeated defiance and the purposeful hurting of another child need to be dealt with immediately, particularly with pre-school children. A well timed smack may prevent a little disobedience from growing into a fully fledged tantrum, or a momentary spitefulness developing into a major battle.

If your child has refused to comply with an instruction that he has clearly understood—for example, 'Turn the TV off!', 'Put your shoes on!', 'Tidy up that mess!'—*repeat* the instruction, *adding the rationale* '. . . because your programme's finished', '. . . because we're going out now', '. . . because we need the table for tea'. If he still refuses, tell him you are going to count to three, after which he will receive a smack if he hasn't done as he was told. This simple technique is amazingly effective, and teaches a child not only that his actions have consequences but that *he* can determine what those consequences will be. Effectively, it places the ball in his court and gives him the choice of whether to play by the rules or to 'commit a foul'—in which case he will have to pay the penalty. This is not so much about imposing discipline as teaching him self-discipline, enabling him to learn through experience that it is more rewarding to do the right thing than the wrong thing.

Recent studies in the USA[3] have confirmed what many parents learn through their offspring anyway—that the most effective way of dealing with recalcitrant or stubborn children is not corporal punishment alone, or reasoning alone, but a combination of reasoning backed up *when necessary* with physical discipline. Don't confuse 'reasoning' with 'debate'—giving a child a reason for your instruction is quite different from allowing him to discuss it with you: that's simply procrastination by another name and as likely as not to end in tears or temper anyway.

If, when you have counted to the dreaded three, the child is still defiant or undecided, deliver the smack quickly, as promised (on the hand, leg or bottom). Never threaten consequences that you are unwilling or unable to carry out, but bear in mind that while a reasonable limit is three smacks, just one may be enough. Do not allow the child to wriggle away from you; tell him to stand still, remind him why he is being smacked, and then do it. If the smack is being given for hurting another child, deliver it in front of the victim—not in order to encourage gloating, but so that justice can be seen to be done. And if the aggressor feels humiliated, so be it: it will be a powerful disincentive to repeating the misdeed. If he is being smacked for defiance, and other children are there, unless they are very young (toddlers) it is better to take him into another room to do the deed—it is hard enough for anyone, adult *or* child, to say sorry, even without an audience. What you have to say will be for his ears only, not for onlookers to revel in. Besides, this way the little one won't have anyone to show off to if he's that way inclined!

After the smack

It may now be appropriate to repeat the instruction but it will sometimes be more effective to turn off the TV or whatever yourself, or to do the task with the child. Then encourage the offender to say sorry either to you or to his victim. This is essential, as it paves the way for an all-important cuddle, which itself demonstrates that it was the behaviour that was unacceptable, not the child that is unloved. This cuddle will not confuse him, as some would claim; rather, it will confirm not only that he is loved, but also that the bad behaviour is forgiven and therefore *finished with*; the relationship is restored, the naughtiness put behind, and everything now carries on as normal.

Children have an amazing and enviable ability to get over upsets and carry on apparently untouched, while at the same time having learnt the lesson that there is great security in obedience. The child who has hurt his playmate should, of course, say sorry to him, and they should then be encouraged to give each other a hug. Young children are actually much better at this than adults—they rarely hold grudges and are generally far more willing to say sorry when they are in the wrong. This facing up to the situation—evident in the demonstration of contrition and forgiveness—gives each child more dignity and more worth, both in their own eyes and in those of their peers. What *they* do, and say, and feel, matters.

No smack given under these circumstances and within these confines should cause any sensible parent to feel guilty about her action or approach. Be confident that what you are doing *and how you are doing it* is for the good of your child, and is helping him to understand not only the right way to act, but also encouraging the right way to think and feel.

There are children for whom a smack (or the threat of one) is effective for a while but then ceases to work. In this case, do not smack harder, however tempting it may be, or more often—*try something else.* Any consistently applied punishment or response that is not achieving the desired result—that is, a change in behaviour or attitude—should be replaced with another. This does not mean that the 'failed' punishment will never again be effective for your child, but simply that it isn't working at the moment. It may well prove invaluable at a later stage or for a different type of naughtiness.

Once a child has reached school age, he will be well on the way to understanding that rules are not there for their own sake, but for specific reasons which generally reflect a concern for an equable life and the good of all. From five onwards, other 'tools' appropriate to the child's age and understanding can be added to the disciplinary kit, and a smack at this age should be very much the exception.

'Bad' smacking

Most of us have, at one time or other, smacked a child when we should not have done—probably our first child, with whom most of our mistakes are made. Equally, most of us have at some time or other smacked harder than we know to be right. The normal reaction in both cases is to feel overcome with guilt and self-loathing and instantly and tearfully to embrace the child, proclaiming how sorry we are for having done it. This is what some childcare professionals are referring to when they say that a smack followed by a cuddle is confusing and potentially damaging to the child; and, of course, given the type of scenario where a parent consistently smacks and immediately apologises for doing so, they are right. But getting it wrong is part of the human condition, as is the hope that enables us to 'pick ourselves up, dust ourselves off and start all over again'. Mistakes are made to be learned from, not to make us give up. If the first time we pranged the car we immediately gave up driving, there would be a lot of very happy environmentalists about and no hole in the ozone layer! But most of us regather our shattered confidence and try again, ensuring that we don't repeat the same mistake and becoming safer and more aware drivers in the process.

The same is true of disciplining our children; whatever tool we use (and smacking is but one of many), we may use it inappropriately or unfairly on occasion, but facing up to the fact that we have got it wrong is the first step towards getting it right next time. Of course, when we do act wrongly, we should say sorry and, if our children are old enough to understand, tell them *why* we were wrong. This is no more than we ask of *them*, and it does children good to see that adults can say sorry too. It may be that *our* temper needs controlling, or that we need to *listen* more and jump to conclusions less. It may mean that we need to pay more attention and make more effort to deal with a situation *before* everything gets out of hand, not after. However we feel we may have messed up, there is always something positive to be salvaged, and the experience of facing up to it can result in a deepening of the parent–child relationship and greater self-knowledge on our part.

Never smacking

The child who is never smacked is possibly a little angel but, more likely, a creature not usually to be found within the pearly gates. Moreover, the parent who never smacks, unless she is largely absent, is likely to be in a chronic state of exhaustion from constantly reasoning, explaining and debating with her ever questioning and never satisfied offspring. Really, of course, all the child wants in certain situations is for the parent to say no and mean it, but the more he pushes at the boundaries set before him the more they give way, and the more they give way, the more he needs to push. This is not a satisfactory state of affairs for the parent or for the child. The parent feels that she is continually compromising, yet the child's behaviour is not improving; the child desperately needs the security of clear boundaries for his behaviour, but what he finds is elasticity and weakness. It is this type of relationship that can lead to unbearable frustration and tension which build up to a sudden eruption of temper, when things may be said or done that are regretted for a long time afterwards.

If a parent refuses to smack when her child behaves badly, but constantly reviews her position in the light of that child's demands, the effect can be even more damaging to both parties as well as to their relationship. A parent who is worn down by constant disobedience will sometimes give up the struggle and opt for a quiet life, giving in to the whining and tantrums and exerting such influence as she can by the use of bribes as rewards for 'good' behaviour. This is no way to train a child and will result in a stubborn and manipulative little person becoming even more so. It clearly is possible to bring up children without ever smacking them. However, most children learn more easily that certain behaviour (spite or defiance, for instance) is unacceptable if they are smacked for it—and sooner rather than later. The momentary pain teaches them more quickly and effectively than an hour's earnest dialogue (or, worse, protracted monologue) ever could.

Adults also need to be aware that while even very young children can understand—and may agree with—simple reasoning, this doesn't mean that they are going to *be* reasonable the next time a conflict arises. So, by all means, give a reason for the action you want, but where that fails to change behaviour, for goodness' sake—and for your child's sake—back it up with something more tangible, and do so quickly. Very often, children who have frequent or prolonged tantrums are those who are not smacked early enough for their misbehaviour, and so the naughtiness, instead of being nipped in

Reasoning is not always appropriate.

the bud, is allowed to escalate until a tantrum results. This is a slow and ineffectual approach to bad behaviour in children and ultimately much more painful and damaging than a swift smack, not only for the child himself but for everyone who comes into the vicinity of the out-of-control little monster.

4 Biting the Bullet: The Truth about Smacking

What a shame—yes, how stupid!—to decide before knowing the facts!
... Any story sounds true until someone tells the other side and sets the
record straight.

—Proverbs 18:13, 17

I first hit trouble with the smacking issue as a childminder in
1992, when I was asked by a social worker, as a condition of
my re-registration under the 1989 Children Act,* to give a
verbal undertaking never to smack a minded child. This I
refused to do, initially because I had discussed discipline with
the mother of the little boy I was looking after, and we were
both agreed that I could smack him if I felt a situation war-
ranted it. From the beginning, I told her if I had smacked him
during the day, and what behaviour and responses had pre-
ceded the smack. Our aim was to offer a united and consistent
front pertaining to all aspects of his growth and development.
I felt very strongly that it is a parent's responsibility to determine how to discipline her own child, and not the role of
the social services or of central government, or indeed of a
childminder, to take over that responsibility in a normal family.

We never actually believed that the threat of deregistration

* All registered childminders had to be re-registered by their Local Authorities
with the introduction of the 1989 Children Act. This included compulsory
attendance of a training course which emphasised, among other things, an
intolerance of any form of discrimination, especially racial and sexual, and
promoted better working partnerships with parents. Most Local Authorities also
asked their 'minders' to give a verbal or written undertaking never to smack
their charges.

would be carried through. It seemed just too ridiculous. As mother and minder we had an excellent relationship, and her son had already become like an extension of my own family: he and my second daughter were almost like twins—indeed, on three occasions, despite the fact that one was blond-haired and the other was brown-skinned I was asked if they *were* twins! However, as the weeks went on it became clear that unless I recanted or compromised—or lied—I would face the shame of being deregistered as a childminder on the grounds that I was 'unfit' to look after children under the age of eight. (By implication that included my own children, then aged three and five.)

I borrowed a copy of the 1989 Children Act from the local library and pored over it, having already established that in British law a parent has not only the right to 'reasonably chastise' her child, but also the right to delegate that responsibility to someone else whom she has chosen. (Had I been a nanny, as opposed to a childminder, the situation would never have arisen since, in the eyes of the law, a nanny is considered exempt from the no-smacking guidelines because she works in the child's own home.) Imagine my surprise when I discovered exactly those two rights enshrined in the introduction to the Children Act.[1] We won the argument, both at the local magistrates' court and then, as a result of the local authority's ill advised appeal, at the High Court in London.

The question remained as to why there was so much official rejection of smacking as a sanction, when every media poll on the subject revealed a huge majority of parents in favour of being able to physically discipline their children. (At the time of the court cases, it must be said, the polls indicated a slightly smaller majority supporting the right of a childminder to smack—and always provided she had permission from the parent.) The National Childminding Association, on the other hand, was adamant that smacking was unnecessary, unprofessional and unwanted by childminders, and claimed that a poll of their members revealed this to be the overriding view of childminders nationwide. Yet inquiries revealed that individual members of the NCMA had not been balloted, but that an emergency resolution had been tabled and a block-voting system had been used.

A survey I sent to all registered childminders in the London Borough of Sutton in November 1992 revealed a contrasting picture, one far more in harmony with national media polls and supporting the stand I had taken. The questions and responses were as follows:

1 Are you a member of the National Childminding Association?	Yes	79%
2 Have you ever been balloted on the 'smacking debate' by the NCMA?	No	89%
3 Do you believe the occasional smack is an effective disciplinary tool?	Yes	82%
4 Have you ever been asked by a parent to smack his or her child?	Yes	45%
5 If a parent did request it, would you be prepared to smack a minded child		
(a) now?	Yes	24%
	Unsure	11%
(b) if current guidelines were relaxed?	Yes	59%
	Unsure	4%
6 Do you believe that a local authority has a moral right to intervene in a private arrangement between a responsible parent and his or her childminder?	No	77%
	Unsure	4%
7 There may soon be legislation making it a criminal offence for a parent to smack his or her own child. Would you agree with this?	No	94%
	Unsure	1%

Perhaps the most significant outcome of the survey was that the analysis of the replies of the few NCMA members who *had* been balloted by the association revealed that *94 per cent believed that a smack was an effective disciplinary tool, and 69 per cent said they would be prepared to smack if the guidelines were relaxed.* Where where *their* views represented in the official NCMA ballot?

So much for smacking being 'unnecessary' and 'unwanted' by childminders. But what about it being 'unprofessional'? Thirty years ago it was commonplace for infant school teachers to give the occasional smack for particularly naughty behaviour. In my experience, teachers who did so were not hated or feared, but regarded with respect and affection by parents and pupils alike. It certainly was not regarded as 'unprofessional' then, in the days when teachers could spend much of their time actually teaching their classes as opposed to trying to control them. I remember only one child in our class of five-year-olds who was smacked by our much loved teacher. He once confided in me—or perhaps 'boasted' would be a more accurate word—that when he grew up he wanted to be a robber! Despite this alarming ambition, the security and discipline of school instilled in him a sense of respect and (relative!) obedience, and by the time he left primary school he behaved no worse than any of the other boys, and probably better than some. Yet if that child were starting school now he would probably be 'excluded' by the age of ten.

'Professional', in its everyday usage, used to imply a degree of learning, knowledge and training and would be applied to people such as doctors, teachers and lawyers. To the extent that today the word is applied more broadly and we have professional bakers and childminders, shopworkers and gardeners, it might be said to have come to mean little more than having a full-time job. If so, then I could be called a 'professional mother'. And since I, in common with most other professional mothers (and most semi-pros), smack my children for certain types of misbehaviour, it is rather derogatory to say that smacking is unprofessional. The most experienced, committed—and successful—childcarers the world over have used this method for countless centuries and, no doubt, will continue to do so.

In view of the overwhelming support of parents for smacking in certain situations, why do the social services professionals so often deny this evidence born of experience? Is it that some are so used, by the very nature of their work, to seeing the worst of family conflict and despair, where parents can't or won't be bothered and where children suffer abuse and neglect, that they cannot distinguish this from the reality of normal family life? Or perhaps some of the most vociferous and determined anti-smackers were themselves physically abused as children? It is a sad and debilitating condition of some adults who were abused that they cannot overcome the long-ingrained fear of any type of physical discipline. They are pathologically incapable, or in some cases unwilling, to distinguish between controlled, loving discipline and uncontrolled, random violence. Their outlook is based on their own subjective experience, and the conflicting yet wider experience of others counts for little in their eyes.

The anti-smacking lobby is led by a pressure group named EPOCH (End Physical Punishment of Children). Their campaign to bring about legal reform is well funded and orchestrated, and enjoys the support of all the Children's Rights pressure groups, amongst others. On what do they base their zeal for the introduction of a legal ban on all smacking? Their four main arguments are as follows:

1 Violence breeds violence, and smacking is violence.
2 Hitting people is wrong, and children are people too.
3 Smacking leads to physical abuse.
4 Smacking doesn't work.

EPOCH claims that its opposition to physical punishment is supported by research evidence, but it is somewhat selective in the research it chooses to back its statements. EPOCH apologists are rather keen on the phrase, 'All the evidence shows that . . .', when what they really mean is 'All the evidence we have chosen to support our case shows that . . .' While we tend to accept this use of 'creative research' from politicians, we don't expect it from people genuinely concerned with the welfare of children and families.

1 Violence breeds violence, and smacking is violence

This first claim is easy to support—up to a point. Research showing that violent prisoners were themselves often the victims of violence or abusive 'discipline' as children will come as no surprise to most.[2] That violence often begets violence is a truism that few would dispute, especially where children are concerned. The particular suggestibility of children was demonstrated by the recent Ninja Turtles craze, when many primary schools were faced with the problem of kicking, aggressive pupils who were aping the antics of their Ninja heroes. Some primary teachers went so far as to say that they could tell from their children's behaviour what they had watched on television the night before. Impressionable children will be influenced by bad examples, and their behaviour will be affected by what they see and hear either immediately around them or on television and video or in computer images.

Where I part company with EPOCH is in their assertion that *smacking* is violence. Violence in a domestic situation, almost by definition, implies the use of force and anger combined with a loss of control and/or respect. Implicit in this is that the violence explodes as a result of the inadequacy of the aggressor rather than because of the actions of the other party. Such violence is both unreasonable and unjustifiable, and the motive behind it—the expurgation of the rage or frustration of the aggressor—entirely selfish. There is no element of fairness or justice here, and that it can seriously be likened to controlled, caring discipline administered by a loving parent in response to a child's deliberate naughtiness, and with the intention of discouraging that bad behaviour, demonstrates an abnormal, even anarchic, concept of both reality and morality. One might as well compare the actions of young car thieves tearing down the motorway in a stolen vehicle with an ambulance crew doing the same thing in their ambulance—the motivation of the first is wicked selfishness, likely to bring disaster or death; the motive of the other is to bring help and relief to *prevent* disaster and death. One key determinant as to whether physical discipline is abusive or not is the motivation prompting the action. Two American paediatricians, Dr Dan Trumball and Dr. S. DuBose Ravenel, have agreed the following distinction between physical discipline and abuse:

	SMACKING	PHYSICAL ABUSE
The act	Smacking: one or two smacks to the buttocks	Beating: to strike repeatedly (also kick, punch, choke)
The intent	Training: to correct problem behaviour	Violence: physical force intended to injure or abuse
The attitude	With love and concern	With anger and malice
The effects	Behavioural correction	Emotional and physical injury

2 Hitting people is wrong, and children are people too
The first thing to note about this assertion is the deliberate use of the word 'hit'. Anti-smacking campaigners can always be identified by their emotive allegiance to this word. It fits easily into the context of violence, anger and lack of control, whereas 'smack' sits more comfortably with the notion of remonstration and discipline. If a group of parents were first asked, 'Do you ever smack your child?', and then, 'Do you ever hit your child?' the two sets of answers would probably be far from identical. There is a much bigger distinction between the words

'smack' and 'hit' in the minds of most parents than is indicated in most dictionaries. If we were to alter the statement to 'We don't smack adults; we shouldn't smack children', it would put us back on the track of discipline as opposed to aggression. No, we don't smack adults; when *they* 'break the rules', other sorts of penalties are incurred, none of which would be helpful or appropriate for a naughty child.

However, there *are* lots of things that we do to children that would probably be considered abusive if applied, other than in a nursing context, to other adults: for instance, we not only wipe noses and knees, but bottoms as well! We wash our children all over, even when they protest that they're not dirty! We put pressure on them to 'eat their greens' and other things they'd rather leave untouched on the plate. We instruct them not to talk when they have food in their mouths and to cover their mouths when they cough. We kiss them better when they're hurt. And so on. We constantly impose our adult will (and wisdom and experience) upon them, even when they are adamantly opposed to it. We treat them as children, not mini-adults.

EPOCH maintains that children need protection from the law because it permits them to be 'reasonably chastised' when they overstep the mark. I suggest that British law, and the vast majority of British parents, are well able to distinguish between reasonable chastisement and abuse. Our children are, in fact, more in need of protection from EPOCH, which would shackle them with all rights and no responsibilities, making them experienced and world-weary before their time, destroying the safety and innocence of childhood and scorning the notion that 'Mummy knows best'. All-knowing, over-indulged, over-experienced children rarely transmogrify into wise or happy adults.

However hackneyed the claim, hard cases *do* make bad law, and a law compromising the responsibilities of the majority because of the wickedness or inadequacy of the few is likely to cause a lot more than just tears before bedtime. According to Ruby Harrold-Claesson, a Swedish lawyer working for the repeal of the Swedish *aga* (anti-smacking law), when the state interferes in the lives of healthy, functioning families, it causes resentment, conflict and compromise. Above all, it destroys the confidence and authority of parents to do what they believe is right and best for their children.

In any case, it is naïve to suggest that anti-smacking legislation would affect the behaviour of those who wilfully abuse children. Such people would continue their depravity in the privacy of their own homes as they do under the present child protection law, using the same intimidation that they have always used: 'This is our little secret, don't tell anyone else . . . they won't believe you anyway . . . they'll take you away', and so forth. The law provides penalties and protection once abusers are caught. Until then it is impotent, and it can never stop those who are determined to commit such crimes.

On this point, EPOCH spokespersons invariably respond: 'A hundred years ago, husbands were allowed to beat their wives, servants and children. Wives and servants are now protected by the law—isn't it about time children were too?' It is perhaps pertinent to point out that some men still beat up their wives today. The law doesn't stop them—it simply provides a penalty when they are reported and prosecuted. Equally, the man who beat his wife would no more have been regarded with respect, honour or affection then than he would be now. To imply that a parent smacking the hand of a naughty four-year-old is in any way comparable with a drunken and vicious thug belting a terrified and defenceless woman because he didn't like his dinner or because his horse came home last, is as indefensible as it is patently stupid.

3 Smacking leads to physical abuse
The view that the real danger of 'a little smack' is that it can escalate into abuse and that therefore the only answer is to ban *all* smacking is akin to stating that since 'a little drink'

can lead to alcoholism, all alcohol should be made illegal. However, according to psychologist Professor H. R. Schaffer, the reality is that this alleged association between ordinary punishment and child abuse is not supported by research.[3] Adults who deliberately abuse children do so because they neither love nor respect their victims, and sometimes take a sick pleasure in the knowledge of their power over such children and in the hurt and fear they can engender in them.

The adult who physically abuses his child because he cannot control his temper constitutes a different case. He may genuinely love his child but nevertheless take out his frustration on him because of his inability to cope with life's pressures. The shame and self-loathing that such a parent experiences can only begin to be healed when he faces up to the reality of the situation, and admits that he is the problem, not the child. For some it may be appropriate to attend an anger-management course, or to talk through with an experienced friend or counsellor alternative strategies for tackling both the child's behaviour and his approach to the child, as well as his own anger management. For some, in the same way as many ex-alcoholics will not touch a drop of alcohol, a self-imposed ban on physical discipline of any kind may be the way forward.

But such cases represent a tiny percentage of parents, and what may be right for them is inappropriate in the vast majority of families. Sure, many parents do reach the end of their tether at some point and wallop a child with more anger than justice, but they *know* when they are guilty of that, and most determine not to do it again and formulate some other strategy should a similar situation recur. This is part and parcel of developing parenting 'skills', and of experience.

One final observation on this point. If it is valid to suggest that smacking leads to physical abuse, surely it would be equally valid to suggest that kissing and cuddling lead to sexual abuse? Any abuse, whatever form it takes, begins not with the hand, but in the head.

4 Smacking doesn't work

This statement is invariably backed up by the rationale that if a child is smacked on any two occasions for the same misdemeanour, clearly the first smack proved ineffectual. Then comes the clincher: 'What do you do when you smack the child harder and he *still* doesn't do what you say ... hit him again, harder and longer?'

My first reaction to this is that the child who needs telling only once about anything has not yet been born. Whatever strategies are employed by parents, all will have to be repeated, not once but many times. Some will be more effective for specific types of behaviour or situation. Some will be more effective for one child than for another. On the few occasions when I have received a parking ticket, I have regretted it and wished that I had spent a little more time looking for a legiti-mate space or returned within the time limit on the meter. Had I *not* been given those tickets, I would be far less careful than I am now. Were the threat of a fine to be relaxed, I might again be tempted to park in an inappropriate way; rules without penalties would effect a bigger moral dilemma than many of us could cope with.

As to what happens when a particular strategy with a certain child doesn't work, the answer isn't *necessarily* more of the same—but it could be. This doesn't mean that a child should be beaten black and blue, or left in his room for two days, or deprived of pudding for a month before the parent finally acknowledges that what she is doing isn't working. It might be that a three-year-old needs an extra smack on his leg to demonstrate that his parent really means business. On the other hand, this might only fuel his determination to remain defiant. Each child is different, and will react differently in different situations. When a particular strategy appears to have no posi-tive effect, rethink the problem and *change the strategy*.

Of course there are wrong ways of smacking—hitting out in anger or frustration; smacking too hard or too often; smacking without giving a warning—just as there can be wrong reasons for smacking, and these may well have negative effects on the behaviour of the children who suffer them. But even small children can testify to the efficacy and fairness of a controlled smack, given within the parameters of a secure and loving relationship. Perhaps the last word on the subject should go to Max, aged three and a half, whose mother had been talking to him about people who felt that smacking was wrong. 'But Mummy,' he responded, 'how will they know when they're *really* naughty if they don't get a smack?'

Who supports EPOCH?

The key names associated with EPOCH include Dr Penelope Leach, Claire Rayner and Peter Newell. Dr Leach, a psychologist and acknowledged childcare guru, has always held strong anti-smacking views; she has publicly stated that she was never smacked as a child and that she has never smacked her own children. She has also stated that 'smacking doesn't work'. Clearly, whatever evidence her comment is based on, it isn't personal experience.

Claire Rayner, ex-children's nurse, agony aunt and author, has spoken and written of the physical abuse she suffered as a child while an evacuee during the war, which may be the cause of her vehement opposition to smacking—'Smacking is violence.' Peter Newell was one of the original directors of the Children's Legal Centre and currently sits as chairman of the Children's Rights Development Unit and the Children's Rights Office. He became the coordinator of EPOCH when the pressure group with which he was previously associated, STOPP (the Society of Teachers Opposed to Physical Punishment), achieved its objective with the banning of corporal punishment in state schools. His partner has worked for some time within the Children's Rights movement, moving from the Children's Legal Centre to the National Children's Bureau.

Although, in its desire to introduce a legal ban on smacking, EPOCH represents only a tiny minority of parents, it enjoys the apparently overwhelming support of childcare professionals. It claims that professional opinion is massively in favour of a legal ban on all physical punishment of children—including moderate and reasonable smacking by parents, within the family home. According to EPOCH, more than sixty major child welfare and other professional groups in the UK 'support the campaign to end all physical punishment by education and legal reform'.

This is an impressive claim—there are some respected names on their list. But are they *really* all calling for legislation against the parental smack? A recent (unpublished) survey has revealed evidence indicating that they are not. All the organisations on its list of supporters with offices in England were contacted by a researcher with a view to asking them four questions on the subject of smacking. The only exceptions were two organisations for whom the National Children's Bureau could not trace an address, and a further three groups who share offices with EPOCH.

The four questions were:

1 When had they adopted an anti-smacking policy?
2 At what level was the policy agreed?
3 On what research was it based?
4 Did their opposition to smacking extend to parents disciplining their own children?

Replies to these questions revealed some surprising information: two organisations stated emphatically that they were not supporters of EPOCH's campaign and would be writing to request the removal of their names from any future published list. Significantly, one of these was a national association of childcare workers which, having taken a decision at its annual conference to support EPOCH, had then individually balloted its members on the smacking issue. Receiving an overwhelmingly negative response to the question of adopting EPOCH's position, it reversed its decision.

A further 12 per cent of organisations, it was revealed, had canvassed grassroots opinion through resolutions at annual general meetings or conferences where activists were prominent in toeing the politically correct line. None had individually balloted their members. Half of the groups surveyed had left policy decisions on this contentious issue to senior members or committees, and a third refused to say how the decision supporting EPOCH had been reached. Concerning *when* each group had adopted its anti-smacking policy, 30 per cent were unable to give a date, and a further 10 per cent admitted they had no written agreement on the matter. Of the remaining 60 per cent, almost all had adopted their anti-smacking position since the launch of EPOCH in April 1989.

What research?

The request for references to research studies which the child-care professionals had found persuasive in reaching their anti-smacking policies (question 3) produced a surprisingly vague response. The organisations that were able to cite specific research in support of their position could be counted on the fingers of one hand, and even these studies related to child abuse rather than to ordinary parental discipline. Several others referred back to EPOCH, including the chairperson of the Children and Families Committee of the influential Association of Directors of Social Services, who wrote: 'I think you will find all the information you need from an organisation called EPOCH.'

A few organisations were honest enough to admit that they had not used any research as a basis for their support of EPOCH. The coordinator of the UK branch of the Defence for Children International stated that the DCI committee that had unanimously agreed to support EPOCH in 1990 had used 'disparate rather than common persuasion. I think other committee members at the time may have reacted emotively rather than informedly (but since such detail would not be in the minutes, there is little point in speculating on what [their reactions] may have been).' Also refreshingly honest was the chairperson of the Children and Families Subcommittee of the British Association of Social Workers, who wrote:

> We are not aware of any research which demonstrates that children who have received physical punishment fare better or worse than others. This is not surprising as such research is notoriously difficult. Given this 'not proven either way' position, however, we do believe that the onus of proof should be on those who favour smacking.

Others may feel that the onus of proof falls on those who wish to criminalise ordinary parents who choose occasionally to use a time-honoured smack as a disciplinary tool to bring their children into line. Nevertheless, this is a tacit admission from a childcare professional who is an avowed supporter of EPOCH that their research has not produced hard evidence to endorse their views.

Should parents be allowed to smack?

Question 4 in the survey relating to whether the organisations on EPOCH's list supported legislation against parents who smack their children brought forth the biggest surprise. A considerable number of the groups replied that parental smacking within the home was outside their brief, and that their opposition to physical correction did not extend beyond their particular professional sphere. So, for example, the National Childminding Association, which is well known for its opposition to smacking by childminders, has no position on the use of smacking by parents. Neither does Kids' Clubs Network, nor the National Association of Nursery Nurses, nor the Daycare Trust, to name a few. The same goes for the relevant committees of the Association of Directors of Social Services and the Association of Metropolitan Authorities; their support for EPOCH on the subject of banning smacking does not extend beyond the spheres of local authority residential and daycare provision. And the Enuresis Research and Information Centre, quite naturally, 'does not have a view on the use of physical discipline for reasons other than bedwetting'.

Then consider the following responses, all of them from officers of groups which purportedly support the campaign 'to end all physical punishment by education and legal reform':

- 'Childline takes no position on whether smacking can be the subject of legislation.'
- 'Not all our members would seek new legislation and we have not had a referendum on the subject ... The British Association for Community Child Health has not committed itself to campaigning for legislation specifically. We would need to canvass members before doing this.'
- 'We [the British Association of Social Workers] recognise that the law currently allows parents to smack children and would wish any legal reform to be considered with great care. Certainly parental smacking of a limited and caring kind should not be criminalised.'

Even the Save the Children Fund, for all its loaded language against smacking in its position statement, recognises that 'this is not an issue to be addressed by legislation but by our society giving positive messages about alternatives to smacking and providing support to parents in the difficult job of bringing up children'.

At the end of the day, only a handful of the groups surveyed, all of which had been listed by EPOCH as being supporters, clearly and unambiguously stated their support for legislation against the parental use of physical discipline. At the very least, this raises serious questions about the integrity of an

Confident Parenting

organisation that makes such impressive-sounding claims. EPOCH should be recognised for what it is: a tiny minority group that does not fully represent the views of childcare professionals, let alone the overwhelming majority of loving parents throughout the UK.

Despite its lack of substantial back-up, EPOCH's influence has permeated all sorts of committees of the great and the good, not least the self-styled Commission on Children and Violence whose report was published in November 1995, and the NSPCC Commission of 1996, both of which called for a change in the law, to give children in all circumstances the same protection against assault as adults. What is meant by this is a legal ban on smacking. The NSPCC two-year study cost over £300,000. In 1993 they made a £3,000 donation to EPOCH. Is this really the way the supporters of the NSPCC expect their donations to be used?

Perhaps the most damaging aspect of the NSPCC report, which claimed that a million children are abused in Britain every year, was that the definition of abuse encompassed everything from a cross word directed at a boy by his mother to the daily rape of a girl by her father. The insensitivity of such a broad definition devalues the appalling suffering of abused children as well as trivialising the whole notion of abuse. One might as well liken a rosy-cheeked schoolchild coming home from school with the familiar refrain, 'I'm starving', to the swollen-bellied, stick-thin child in Rwanda whispering the same words to the aid worker. The comparison is obscene, incomprehensible and unforgivable.

Sweden: children's Utopia or social deception?

Sweden is the child-loving nation much lauded by representatives of EPOCH because of its famous anti-smacking legislation of 1979. It is presented as a moral Utopia where children are no longer 'hit', and where parents have been re-educated to understand that there are always better alternatives to smacking. Yet Sweden has the highest suicide rate in Europe amongst children and young people; the deaths of children as young as six and seven are reported to be included in these statistics. Groups of older Swedish children have been banned from some skiing resorts in Austria and the French Alps because of their disruptive behaviour. Many Swedish towns experience noisy, drunken teenagers disturbing the peace in the evenings. The Stockholm subway is one of the most vandalised in the world. These are poor indicators of a society at ease with itself.

The year after the introduction of the Swedish anti-smacking legislation a cross-cultural study revealed that Swedish parents were less likely to smack their children than were American parents. However, they were twice as likely to beat them up. Overall, there were no appreciable differences in the rates of abusive, violent acts as between Sweden and the US.[4] More recent studies have revealed that 4 per cent of Swedish parents still use 'grave forms of violence'[5] towards their children. Stockholm University concurs that the incidence of serious physical punishment is the same in Sweden as in the USA. It would appear that, despite all the rhetoric, the Swedish experiment has failed to reduce the rate of serious child abuse.

What about ordinary parents? In 1991 the respected Swedish Opinion Research Institute (SIFO) conducted a poll to commemorate the twelfth anniversary of the anti-smacking law. Thirty-five per cent of the mothers polled deemed it right and proper to use some kind of physical punishment on their children, and a further 35 per cent were thought to hide their true feeling on the subject.

EPOCH has frequently claimed that, despite the fears and protests of pro-smacking campaigners, since the Swedish legislation of 1979 only one parent in Sweden has been prosecuted: a father who was fined £10 for spanking his eleven-year-old son.[6] This could be described as being economical with the truth on a massive scale, and at least one British newspaper has rushed to publish the assertion without bothering to check the facts.[7] The truth is that there are no figures for the number of parents who have been prosecuted for smacking their children, or for the number of children taken into care because their parents have smacked them. However, lawyers working for families in Sweden state that 'hundreds of parents have been prosecuted for domestic squabbles with their children', and claim to be investigating hundreds of cases of parents having 'lost' their children to the state. Twenty-five thousand children are believed to have been forcibly removed from their homes. There are currently six cases pending in the European court, and one pro-family solicitor alone has a further twenty cases on her books.

The discrepancy between these claims and the apparent outcome of the anti-smacking law, and the lack of statistics, are explained partly by the Swedish courts' refusal to distinguish physical punishment from child abuse and assault and battery. Hence, accused parents are not prosecuted under the 1979 anti-smacking (civil) law, but under the criminal law. Social services have the right to remove a child from the custody of his parents, without prior notice, on the strength of an anonymous allegation that one of the parents has smacked him. Such a child can be placed in a foster home, to which access by the parents may be severely restricted. Sometimes there is a ban on parents' visiting rights, and even telephone and letter contact may be forbidden. The number of suicides and attempted suicides among children and teenagers taken into care is high, even for Sweden.

Such are the claims of those fighting to repeal the Swedish anti-smacking legislation.

Simone Ek, a spokesman for a Swedish children's charity, has stated: 'All our children know that their parents cannot hit them', but Swedish law also prohibits parents from sending an unruly child to his room; this would be considered 'degrading treatment' and, as such, is also punishable. According to lawyer Ruby Harrold-Claesson, 'Swedish parents have no rights in their own homes; they dare not correct their children for fear that they might be reported. The law is directed against the family.' Anna Christensen, Professor of Civil Law at Lund University, has said that courts are too quick to believe a child's word against the parents'. Katarina Runske, president of the Swedish Family Campaign Foundation, believes that the state's interference in how parents care for their children has actually led to neglect. It seems that, once you take away parents' rights, some will abandon their responsibilities too.

This nightmare of administrative violence is played down by the Swedish government and by the press, which is, unknown to many Swedes, subsidised by the state.

Why is Sweden so important? Part of the answer is that other countries that are under pressure to adopt anti-smacking policies look to Sweden to see how such a policy has worked there. If it could be shown that children's behaviour and the stability and quality of family life have improved since the imposition of the ban on physical punishment, there would be a stronger case for giving it further careful consideration. If the incidence of child abuse could be demonstrated to have fallen, that would constitute even more compelling evidence for other countries to consider changing their own law, even if it were against the wishes and instincts of a majority of the population. The empirical evidence which indisputably supports such a change in the law is in short supply in this case, unlike similar problems involving a change in social attitude. (The compulsory use of seatbelts in all vehicles is a comparable case.) A recent research project in Canada revealed that 30 per cent of interviewees would support a proposed ban on physical discipline. However, that figure increased to 65 per cent when they were asked if they would support such a law if it could be proved to reduce injuries to children.[8]

Advocates of the Swedish experiment make exactly this

claim, but seem unable to produce the statistics to back it up. Can it be that the reality in progressive, liberal Sweden doesn't actually stand up to too close an inquiry? For all our sakes, and especially for our children's, the claim that the banning of physical discipline would reduce the number of injuries inflicted on children must be subjected to more balanced, independent and honest scrutiny than has so far been demonstrated by EPOCH or by any of the other Children's Rights activists. There is some study evidence that suggests that abolishing or reducing rates of ordinary parental smacking fails to reduce physical child abuse and may in fact increase it.[9] The final word on Sweden must go to lawyer Ruby Harrold-Claesson:

> The law against the physical punishment of children is dangerous and must be repealed because it does more harm to children than a spanking from mother or father. When the authorities—social or police—intervene in the life of a well functioning family, its life is destroyed. There is nothing that can mend the hurt and pain and bitterness that the authorities cause, and the children are the losers.

It is relatively easy to do research that sets out to prove a certain viewpoint—'violence breeds violence' is a prime example. Some psychologists will try to use such research to prove something quite different: for example, that loving physical discipline can result in violent delinquents. The problem is that, because of the huge complexity of the smacking issue, responsible, balanced research is much more difficult to carry out. The variables that need to be taken into account include the closeness (or otherwise) of the parent–child relationship; the frequency of physical punishment; its severity; its prominence (whether it is the main means of discipline or one of many); whether it is used in conjunction with reasoning; the age of the child and his perception of the legitimacy and consistency of the disciplinary methods used.[10] Short-term

analysis has to determine whether the punishment is effective—
does it inhibit or stop the behaviour it is intended to deter? And
long-term analysis must determine whether any long-term
damage, emotional or psychological, has been inflicted on
adults who received normal—that is, non-abusive—physical
punishment as children.[11]

The respected American psychologist Diana Baumrind
wrote in 1996:

> Prudently used, spanking can effectively accomplish its
> limited goals with less harm, and often more successfully,
> than alternative disciplinary tactics. Prudent use of physi-
> cal punishment in a family setting is no more a generative
> form of aggression in parents or children than getting out
> of bed in the morning is a generative cause of getting hit
> by a drunk driver . . . the key to preventing societal viol-
> ence lies elsewhere . . . the generative causes . . . are
> primarily the hopelessness and helplessness resulting
> from social neglect of family problems associated with
> persistent poverty, and secondarily societal failure to
> deter and punish expressions of destructive aggression
> promptly, severely and fairly.[12]

There is an increasing body of research suggesting that a
blanket prohibition of all parental smacking would be counter-
productive, an overly simplistic attempt at solving the problem
of child abuse. Psychologist Dr Robert Larzelere concluded
in his overview of studies researching the parental practice of
physical discipline that 'The most important finding of the
review is that there are not enough quality studies that docu-
ment detrimental outcomes of nonabusive physical punishment
to support advice on policies against the age-old parental practice.'[13] The need for better-conducted studies on parental use
of physical discipline is generally agreed, particularly on the
distinction between abusive and beneficial forms of corporal
punishment. It has been recognised, even by those basically

opposed to physical punishment, that appropriate use of smacking is the most effective way of backing up other disciplinary techniques,* and that it is particularly effective when combined with reasoning.[13, 14] Guidelines suggested by those who support appropriate use of physical punishment include:

- that the smacking be limited to two or three slaps with an open hand;
- that the child be between the ages of eighteen months and six years;
- that smacking be used to supplement positive parenting, not to replace it;
- that smacking be used primarily to back-up less aversive discipline, such as verbal correction or time out.

Those who frame our laws need to do so from informed decisions based on honest research. On such a crucial and emotive issue as discipline within the family, policy-makers would do well to listen to the voices of the majority of caring, loving parents and to those experts whose academic and scientific studies substantiate that wisdom and experience.

---

* All professionals in Sweden had agreed during the late 1970s that 'corporal punishment was a bad method of childrearing' but 'it eliminated unwanted behaviours in animals and humans more quickly than any other method'.

Part Two

LIVING WITH CHILDREN

The first part of this book is largely about theory as opposed to reality; principles as opposed to practice. The reality of parenthood, as described in Part Two, sometimes complements the dream, but often it brings a rude awakening when high-minded ideals and agreed principles too easily dissolve into what is practical and expedient. Adopting a pragmatic approach to family life is not an admission of failure, however, but more likely to result in the development of a healthy, positive parent-child relationship in which both are encouraged to succeed but allowed to fail (and try again) without being hamstrung by unrealistic expectations or preconceived ideals.

If you are expecting your first child, don't tramline yourself too determinedly with a resolve to stick, come what may, to what are as yet untried principles. Initial goals are best limited to getting through the day! Most of us are only too well aware that life 'after baby' will never be the same again, and some begin to wonder how on earth they will cope, even before the 'bump' begins to show. Others have very firm ideas, well before their child is born, about the type of parent they want to be. They focus on one particular aspect, perhaps deciding that they will do things the traditional way—for example, by using 'terry' nappies instead of disposables. As their child grows older they will cope with the inevitable naughtiness with a mixture of love and logic, and being competent parents will soon iron out any temper tantrums that occur along the way. If only it was as simple as that!

Given time and experience, the practice of parenting may differ significantly from some of the principles that, as pre-parents, we espouse so warmly. Anyone nervously cradling her first-born is unlikely to imagine herself ever being cross with that tiny, helpless bundle, and a fierce, protective anger would probably arise at the mere thought of *smacking* such a tiny treasure. Yet a mere two years or so later, many parents will be adjusting their early ideals, learning through experience that a smack is the most effective way of dealing with some types of naughtiness.

Part of the purpose of this book is to give parents the confidence to follow their best instincts in the way they discipline their children, and not to be compromised by the particular 'political correctness' which decrees that to smack is to fail. By exploring the concept of 'discipline' with all its many permutations, including the rights and wrongs of smacking, I hope to provide the evidence both to back up the conviction that it can be the right thing to do, and also to defuse the arguments of the well-meaning but politicised parenting advisers who maintain that 'smacking' is *always* wrong. Happy parenting!

5   From Birth to Eighteen Months

A whole new ball game

Some mothers take instantly to their new-born babies—especially the first. For others of us, cradling our first-born is the first step on a survival course that will lead into totally uncharted waters and take us physically, emotionally and mentally to the very limit of our endurance.

My first daughter arrived tiny (under five pounds), hungry (my placenta had packed up) and very, very cross. Somehow she knew that she had been short-changed in the food department and was determined that it wouldn't happen again. Unfortunately, as we were both complete novices at breast-feeding our best efforts met only minimal success, and by the end of our first forty-eight hours' acquaintance we were both exhausted and entirely disenchanted with each other. Not a promising start to our future relationship.

I remember sitting in the maternity ward washed out and with all hope gone, having tried—and failed—once again to feed this desperate baby. Suddenly, she looked vaguely but—or so it seemed to me—accusingly in my direction, opened her perfect rosebud mouth and dropped her lower jaw, which then shook violently as the most piteous cry emanated from that unsatisfied orifice. (We later called it the 'bottom lip tremble'.) At the time it was all I could do to pick her up, thrust her at my husband and burst into tears. I then turned to see my beaming mother and sisters-in-law advancing down the ward, to inspect the latest member of the family and congratulate the competent and capable new mother. At this point I wished not that she, but that *I*, had never been born.

It did get better. We persevered with breast-feeding and finally got the hang of it. The problem then became that, having found her fount of life, baby Abbey became extremely reluctant to let it go. Soon learning that it was unwise (not to speak of painful) to attempt to pull her off, I resigned myself to letting her remain 'plugged on' each time until she fell asleep. As she wasn't a particularly sleepy baby, this meant that I spent an abnormally sedentary week or so before a passing midwife recognised the problem and shared with me her technique for disengaging even the most determined infant. Having had her vice-like grip broken did not please this angry and still hungry baby, and it was shortly after learning the knack of detachment that we renamed her Abiwail.

Abbey had a voracious appetite, but by the end of each day I had very little milk left; she then wanted to stay latched on because she was genuinely hungry. I had been told that the body would supply as much milk as the baby required and that all I needed to do was follow a healthy diet and remember that I was still eating for two. It would have been a lot more useful to have been advised to drink extra fluid to help the body lactate more efficiently. Whatever the manuals say, not all women naturally produce all the milk their child needs, and little tips such as 'Drink more' can make all the difference to a hungry and fractious baby and a sore and weary mother. I was also belatedly advised to 'top her up' with formula milk in the evening if she wasn't satisfied. In fact, Abbey put on weight extremely quickly, which was why the baby clinic showed no concern, but their response might have been different if the clinic had been held in the evening when she was screaming for more and I was flat-chested and empty. It was a great relief for both of us when her twelfth week approached and we could add the first solids to her liquid diet.

It was during those first three months that I experienced

extreme fatigue, frustration, desperation and *anger* towards my tiny daughter. She seemed to be always hungry, never satisfied and was often wailing, and I didn't know how to help or stop her. My lack of confidence must have communicated itself to her, for when we went out as a family she often seemed happier if her daddy held her, and when we went to see my mother-in-law I would thankfully pass her over into grandma's eager arms and watch confounded as she coaxed gummy grins from Abbey before eventually rocking her confidently to sleep. God bless all grandmas everywhere!

During those first three months I was aware of a great sense of responsibility towards the seemingly disgruntled little creature I had brought into the world, but there was no corresponding feeling of love and I did often wonder at my lack of maternal feeling. In the course of the second three months, however, I found that I was looking forward to her smile and enjoying *her* enjoyment (especially of food!), and excited by the things that interested and excited her. Love was growing. It had taken a while to start, but by the time Abbey's first sister was about to make her entrance two years later I was guiltily wondering how I should ever be able to love this second child as much as the first.

Pleasant dreams!

The first three months of a baby's life are arguably the toughest period for parents, especially for the mother. Not only does every waking moment revolve around him—why is he crying? does he need changing? has he got a temperature? should I call the doctor? how long will he sleep? will the hoover wake him up? and so on—but so do too many would-be sleeping moments too! Yet even while the night feeds are still too many and too frequent, little things can be done to help establish a routine that will be beneficial to both mother and child. When he wakes at night, feed him as quietly as possible and without putting on a bright light—a subdued landing or hall light will do, or even a street light if a window is near. If he needs changing, do it as quickly and calmly as possible—no raspberries on tummies in the middle of the night—and again, with as little light as is practical. Babies do not have a natural awareness of day and night, but we can encourage this to develop by keeping the hours of darkness as peaceful and unstimulating as possible.

Many babies begin sleeping through the night at around three to four months. Until this longed-for breakthrough they usually wake for a feed every four hours or thereabouts. If, however, your baby is consistently waking every couple of hours, having a quick feed and then going off again, this little person is probably doing so because it is nice and has become a habit, not because he is hungry. It is important to knock some habits on the head before they become really established— and this is one of them. Provided that your baby is healthy and developing normally, he will come to no harm if ignored for a couple of hours even if he finally cries himself to sleep, and even if he screams solidly for the whole two hours. Of course, the object of the exercise is twofold: to train the baby to sleep longer between feeds and to enable his parents to sleep longer between feeds! A screaming, frustrated infant will not understand why he has been left, but there are some things that can be learnt without understanding.

However, few mothers could bear to hear their child scream for so long, even if there was no one else in the house to disturb. So the solution is to give the babe a good last feed, and then put him in his pram or carry-cot in the room that is furthest away from your bedroom and has as many doors as possible between you and it. Shut all the intervening doors. Don't lie in bed straining to hear every last whimper; remind yourself that he's not hungry, dirty or ill, put a pillow over your head if necessary and *go to sleep*. It's amazing how the guilt and anxiety induced by a screaming baby roll away when you can't hear him. And when, fearing that he has screamed himself to death, you go down in the morning (or when the alarm sounds four hours later) yet find him sleeping sweetly, you may even manage to persuade yourself that you did the right thing. There are times when it pays to be a little selfish, especially when there are other children to consider. Mothers of young babies *need* their sleep; healthy babies *need* regular feeds—but not every two hours.

This process may have to be repeated for three or four days, but it will work—for the benefit of all concerned.

Sometimes we actually encourage babies to sleep lightly by picking them up the instant they murmur. Babies, like the rest of us, sometimes call out in their sleep or half wake before going back into a deeper sleep. To be picked up and inspected when they are in that no-man's-land between waking and sleeping does nothing to inspire them to sleep, and everything to help them wake. Also, they become dependent on the reassuring warmth of the cuddle to help them return to their slumber, rather than making that little journey on their own.

Encouraging your baby to sleep longer and more easily at night is also helped by 'putting him down' at a regular time each evening and establishing a routine that he will come to recognise as preceding 'sleepy time'. A bath or wash and a nappy change followed by a relaxed feed and cuddle make a useful start. Feeding in a dim light (as mentioned earlier), rocking gently and talking or singing softly, or listening to very quiet music (not heavy metal!) all enhance that restful atmosphere and help your baby to relax and rest. Some babies seem to sleep better if the music is left playing after the parent has left the room; a radio left on very low can have an equally soporific effect and may serve to fool him into thinking that he is not alone!

There are times when we parents *know* our baby is tired and needs a sleep, yet he fights it with every ounce of his fractious energy. This is especially noticeable in summertime, when all the windows are open and it seems that all the world must be able to hear your shrieking infant! My first child, born in May, was just such a baby—and summer came early that year. The only thing that helped was a suggestion from the special-care midwife who visited because Abbey had been so small. Her advice was to wrap her up securely in a muslin nappy (she was that tiny) so that her arms were held by her sides and her legs unable to kick. Far from fighting against the restraint, she seemed to find security in her immobilisation, and usually stopped protesting in a matter of minutes. As she got bigger we used a soft crocheted blanket through which she would curl her baby fingers and which, although equally secure, had greater elasticity than the muslin. Perhaps the soft security of the blanket reminded her somehow of the womb—anyway, it offered her (and us) great comfort. When she became more settled and found sleeping less of a battle, we first wrapped her more loosely and then simply laid the blanket over her as she was put in her cot. The blanket itself had become her comfort; it no longer had to *do* anything—being there was enough. Wrapping a baby up in this way may be unusual these days, but in former times it was done as a matter of course—we all know of one particular baby who was 'wrapped in swaddling clothes and laid in a manager'.

Sleeping together

Most parents tend to start off with the baby sleeping in their room, for obvious and very practical reasons. However, once the babe is sleeping through the night fairly regularly, he is usually moved to the 'nursery'. If there are older siblings it may well be worth considering sleeping him with them rather than separately. In my experience, babies who sleep alone tend to wake at the slightest sound. But put them in with another child or two, and after a settling-in period (only a few days) they seem to sleep more soundly than before *and* be less demanding when they wake in the morning. Hearing the sound of breathing and the inevitable movement of their older brothers or sisters seems to have a reassuring and calming effect. And getting attention from a sibling is infinitely preferable to waking alone, even if it isn't quite as good as having Mummy there.

As far as the older child or children are concerned, a snuffling, crying baby is as a flea to a cat—initially disturbing but very quickly taken for granted, irritation forgotten. One big advantage of children sharing a room is that they very quickly develop the ability to sleep through anything—not only each other's coughs and midnight visits to the loo but also emergency sirens, fireworks, and thunder and lightning. Which all makes life a lot easier for the tooth fairy and Father Christmas when they have to call! And in the morning they'll play or chat together *if that's what they are expected to do*, rather than disturbing Mummy and Daddy.

Great expectations

Expectations have a significant part to play in the developing understanding between parent and child. Children can be trained to play quietly in their bedrooms in the morning, and as they get older they are able to understand that they mustn't just burst in on Mummy and Daddy, but knock first or wait until they are invited in for a cuddle. One house-rule we have found invaluable is that the children don't go downstairs in the morning until we are up. If they're playing in the bedroom you know there's only so much mischief they can get up to.

Night-lights

Many parents use a night-light in the children's room. I have never done so because mine have always slept perfectly well in darkness. And I have a theory that night-lights may cause as many problems as they solve. It is surely more likely that little imaginations will conjure up monsters from just discernible shapes and shadows than from complete darkness. Leaving the door ajar could create similar difficulties, in addition to tacitly encouraging older children to call out. There is something very final about shutting the bedroom door on young children, but it is a finality that can be reassuring in its unmistakableness—the day is now over, the time for sleep is come.

Dulcet tones

Babies need not only to be cuddled, fed, watered and have their nappies changed, but also to be talked to. It doesn't matter that they don't understand—it is the tone of voice they will respond to, not the meaning of the words. It doesn't really matter what you say, either—it could be French verbs or timestables for that matter! Having a baby is a great opportunity to work at loosening inhibitions and overcoming reserve—a baby is not going to criticise what you say or how you say it. For those who lack confidence in their own opinions and need encouragement to speak out, a baby is an unbeatable opportunity to do just that. Whether he is being dressed, changed, fed, taken to the shops or whatever else, tell him about his world (the colours, the weather, plants, animals, people, what he's having for dinner).

It is impossible to talk too much to a baby! When he's looking at books, make the pictures come alive. Again, it doesn't matter that he doesn't understand what you're saying—the important thing is that he's hearing language and sharing a closeness and involvement with the person he loves and trusts above all others. The more he hears, the more quickly his understanding will grow, and the more he will want to communicate back to you. Make language fun by introducing him to amateur dramatics. Develop a range of funny voices to use with word games and rhymes—'This little piggy went to market', 'Round and round the garden like a teddy bear'—and make up your own songs and rhymes. Become adept at farmyard impersonation—'What does duck/ cow/frog say?'—and remember your own favourite nursery rhymes and *sing* them to your captive audience! It doesn't matter if you can't remember all the words or the right tune, or if you've never been able to sing in tune anyway. Baby won't be any the wiser, and it won't retard any latent musical ability that he may have inherited from his other parent.

At bath time teach him the parts of his body—'Show me your nose!' and so on—but do it slowly, one feature at a time and, most of all, make it fun. It doesn't matter if baby gets it wrong, if he tells you that a sheep says 'moo' or points to his toes when asked for his nose. Just laugh with him, but then tell him what the right sound or part is. When he gets it right let him know—by the tone of your voice, the expression on your face, the enthusiasm of your hands (clap!). Exaggerate everything, relax, and *enjoy* your baby. An infant who is used to laughter and laughing, who learns that *he* can contribute both to the word-play and to the laughter, will be a happier, easier to manage child than one who is not given those wonderful learning opportunities.

Abstract concepts

Before a baby is crawling there isn't an awful lot he can do to be deliberately naughty; a certain amount of mobility is required for disobedience to flourish! However, that doesn't mean that he should not hear the word 'No' now and again. When my middle daughter was well under a year she discovered a fascination for a little red spot on my neck, and tried to pick it off on more than one occasion. Much as I would have liked to lose this hereditary wart, I didn't feel this was quite the way to go about it. She became very used to hearing 'No' and having her hands removed from my neck, and she eventually learned that if she did not stop she would be put down or passed to somebody else.

Many babies have a fascination for faces and hair, and some take a peculiar pleasure in scratching one or pulling the other. Before this becomes too ingrained a habit, it is useful to teach the meaning of the word 'gentle'. This is not achieved by screaming 'Be gentle!' at a delighted baby triumphantly brandishing his handful of hair, but rather (after wiping the tears or blood from your face) by saying the words in a gentle, onomatopoeic tone while softly stroking his arm or face. Allow him to do the same to you but respond firmly if he begins to be less than gentle. A baby cannot learn the meaning of an abstract word or concept without an appropriate action to illustrate or explain it. Follow through the lesson by taking one of his favourite toys and 'loving' it gently; then ask the (hopefully penitent) child if he would like to do the same. When teddy goes hurtling across the floor you know you haven't quite got the message across but, gently retrieving and comforting teddy, console yourself with the knowledge that Rome wasn't built in a day and at least you've made a start.

Wrigglers

Some babies are more wriggly than others! But even with the no-worse-than-average wriggler there are times when life is a lot easier if he can be persuaded to stop squirming for a minute or two, if only when he's having his nappy changed. Efficiently changing a smelly nappy when the determined infant is practising his kung fu technique or demonstrating the latest in roly-polies is not for the faint-hearted or for mere mortals with only one pair of hands. In my experience a really determined squirmer *never* responds to parental pleadings, and rarely acknowledges facial expression or tone of voice. The only thing to do, having said no in as firm a tone as you can muster, is to give him a sharp tap on his leg with your fingers. This will probably give you only a couple of seconds before he vents his ear-splitting wrath at such treatment, but it's amazing what one can accomplish in that brief instant. The benefit of that tap on the leg will only be appreciated in subsequent changings, when baby will be more inclined to respond to your expression and tone of voice, postponing the next gymnastics session until he is clean and dry once again. He may need occasional reminders for as long as he is wearing nappies, but that is a small price to pay for a generally quick and easy change time. When he does, at your request, stop the wiggly-worm impersonation, reward him with your approval in a way that he can understand—smile or laugh at him, kiss him, say 'Good boy!' 'That's better!' 'Well done!'. In addition to training him to keep still(ish) while he is being changed, this is also teaching him that no is a word not to be ignored and that it carries unpleasant consequences if it *is* ignored.

Just as it is never too soon to talk to a baby, so it is never too early for him to *experience*—understanding comes later—that words and actions can have positive or negative consequences. In the first few months a young child learns exclusively through experience: he is hungry or uncomfortable, so he cries and is fed or comforted. His action has provoked a response. When he gurgles or grasps for things, someone appears and talks to him or gives him something to hold. His responses have consequences which he may not understand but which he nevertheless learns to expect. Confusion and frustration set in if those consequences are not consistent; in the wriggly-baby scenario it is pointless to give him a tap at one nappy change only to ignore his horizontal jiving at the next. Consistency helps a child to understand the expected norms of any particular circumstance.

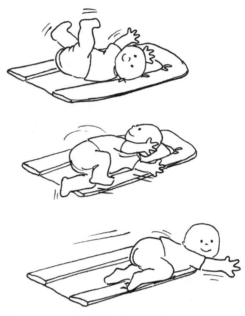

Demonstrating the latest in roly-polies.

Crawlers

Once babies start to crawl or 'bottom-shuffle' you know you've *really* got to watch out. As they have no innate knowledge of what is dangerous or of great value, it is crucial to keep not only medicines, detergents and so on in a safe place, but also any Ming vases or other breakable heirlooms you may have lying around! All the same, I believe that it's a mistake to remove absolutely everything that baby might reach simply because it is breakable. How is he to learn not to touch certain things if there is nothing he must not touch? Equally, how is he to learn to treat certain objects carefully if he never has the chance to handle them? It boils down to two things: teaching your child to respect the word 'No', and developing either a sixth sense or eyes in the back of your head.

Teaching respect for 'No' begins with the way the word is said. There are children who respond so well to a firm tone of voice that they never need any further disincentive to stop their unwanted behaviour. However, such children are few and far between! Most need, from time to time, more than verbal instruction alone to keep them on the straight and narrow. When your newly mobile baby first attempts to explore the video player, the toilet seat or an older sibling's collection of pogs, the initial response should clearly be 'No', followed if necessary by the prompt removal of the babe from the object of desire—except in the latter instance, where the older child might be persuaded to give him one of her precious pogs. Should the insistent little pickle immediately return to the scene of temptation, repeat the procedure. However, if he is still intent on the forbidden territory, more drastic action is required. This may involve removing him to another room or putting the adult imagination into gear and finding something suitably fascinating with which to distract him. (Keys are always a good bet, providing you remember to get them back again.) Yet some babies are so single-minded that not even keys will distract them, and this is where the teaching of consequences needs to be brought back into play.

When a toddler has determinedly and repeatedly ignored 'No', then the time comes to back up the word with unmistakable action. One day, when my first baby, aged about nine months, was careering about in her baby-walker and had reached for the nth time for something that was potentially harmful, I remember asking her 'Mummy smack?' She looked at me and then went for the object again. Moving over to her, I said 'Mummy smack' and tapped her hand. She looked at me as if to say 'What was that?', then went again for the same object. This time I said 'Mummy smack' and smacked her pudgy little hand quite sharply—just once. She didn't like it—but she didn't go back to the banned object, either. Significantly, after that episode she responded in exactly the same way to the word 'No'—that is, she ignored it!—but when faced with the question 'Mummy smack?' she almost always backed down and reacted positively, obediently, to what she was being told. Even more significant, once a rule had been established, she accepted it and did not test it again, even when she was not being watched.

I returned to teaching when Abbey was seven months old, and was very fortunate in having my mother-in-law to look after her. Grandma loved having Abbey, and to my eternal shame consistently noticed new teeth (even the first one) before I did, and when Abbey was tired would rock her to sleep as a matter of course—something that I never acquired the knack of doing. However, there did come a wondrous day when Grandma admitted to having had a *small* problem, and all over a bowl of oranges. Her little granddaughter was very fond of oranges, and grandma used to give her one most days after lunch. However, the ever hungry and impatient Abbey didn't like grandma's ideas of timing *or* rationing, and started to help herself. Grandma began finding oranges in all sorts of odd places, and all with tiny teeth marks in the skin. Having firmly and repeatedly said 'No', but to no avail, she then removed the fruit-bowl from its usual place for a few days, only to find on its return that the irresistible attraction had not diminished. So she placed the oranges on a high shelf where they could be seen but not reached. Or so she thought. When she found Abbey attempting to climb the shelves on the wall, she recognised that the oranges were a problem.

The solution to the seemingly intractable problem was a simple one—an old-fashioned, tried and tested smack. Every time Abbey touched the oranges after Grandma had said 'No', she received a smack on the hand. It took a couple of days, after which she lost interest in the fruit but had her confidence restored in Grandma's timing! She still loved oranges, she still loved her grandma, but the 'No' lesson had been reinforced and Abbey had learnt that the word had both meaning *and consequences*, even when used by Grandma! She was about a year old at the time.

Driven to distraction

Distraction can be a very useful technique for dealing with babies and toddlers when they are hurt, frightened or frustrated. The basic purpose of distraction is, after all, to take their minds off whatever has upset them. Baby bumps can be kissed better; sudden fears can be cuddled away; tiny tantrums can be instantly forgotten by the introduction of something more interesting into the field of play. This might be as simple as pointing out a bird close to the window, or showing the child the leaves moving on a tree as the wind blows through them. Some children who have become very agitated indoors will calm down almost miraculously when taken outside; whether it's the freshness of the air or the hugeness of the world, I don't know—it just happens. Other useful distractions include the production of an object the child is not usually allowed to play with: one of my toddlers could be placated with a nappy in a paper bag! Another loved to pull a tissue to bits—clearing up the mess together afterwards was a small price to pay. Equally effective can be the playing of a familiar tape (words or music); or, *very* occasionally, the bribe of chocolate buttons (the more health-conscious can substitute raisins or sultanas). I am not a great fan of bribery but it can have its uses, and with small children there are definitely times when discretion is the better part of valour!

As a general rule, I don't believe distraction is often an appropriate way of dealing with actual *disobedience*. It may help resolve a situation in the short term, but all the parent is doing here is changing the subject (sweeping the dust under the carpet, if you like). Distracting a child from deliberate defiance will not teach him that a certain behaviour or attitude is wrong and should therefore not be repeated, nor will it afford the opportunity to emphasise the importance of 'being good'. How can a child learn to *choose* to be good if he is not told that certain things are bad, naughty or off limits? Such a child will be good more by luck than by judgement, and while luck is welcome it's the judgement we need to encourage. I believe that patiently removing a determined child, time after time after time, from something or somewhere that is out of bounds, is counter-productive as far as teaching discipline is concerned. Both parent and child may well end up extremely stressed, in a situation that could have been definitively resolved hours earlier but which instead has been allowed to evolve into a battle of wills. The child may eventually capitulate—on this occasion—but how much more easily, quickly and efficiently he would have learnt the same lesson had he received a tap on his chubby hand reinforcing the first 'No' when he initially set out to test the limits prescribed for him.

The art of exchange

Fairly frequently, tiny children manage to get hold of things that they shouldn't—grandad's glasses, big sister's marbles, fat slug from the garden, and so on. Persuading them to relinquish these could be likened to asking a lottery winner to give up his ticket. However, a little diplomacy can go a long way. Experience has taught me never to try to remove from a child any deliciously illegal treasure without having an alternative immediately to hand. Bartering is the name of the game—it sometimes helps if the 'swap' object is close to the original in form (for instance, a sibling's toy sunglasses for Grandad's specs), but what can one offer in exchange for a *slug*? The answer may be a bit of time and attention—'Lets put him back in his house under this leaf and do some digging over here'; or the promise of water—'Put that sticky old slug down and we'll wash your hands with the watering-can/bucket/hose.'

Some toddlers, and older children too, are drawn to water like ducks to a pond, and the promise of a good splash will induce them to give up almost anything.

Sometimes a child will not be persuaded to have his booty taken from him even for the most generous exchange, but he may be willing, rather than let you do it, to *put it back himself*. Equally, he may be quite happy to return the item to its rightful owner, rather than give it to an intermediary. My third daughter would usually be content to return her pilfered trophies to a 'special place' (top of the television or a shelf in the sideboard), even without an exchange. Then she had her reward in the approval—'Well done!', '*Good* girl!'—that followed.

Given the best will and motivation in the world on your part, there are still times when a baby or toddler won't respond to your machinations and you do have to firmly remove something from him, or him from something. The ensuing paddy is best dealt with by either distracting him or putting him in his cot for a few minutes if he shows no signs of calming down. In the latter case, although he may initially scream even louder as you leave him, he will probably be so glad to see you a few minutes later that he will allow you to cuddle and calm him. Should this strategy fail, you have to harden your heart, return him to his cot and repeat the whole process. If the emotional stress bubbling through your arteries reaches too high a level, *recognise it, admit it, and leave baby in his cot* until he stops screaming or cries himself to sleep *or* until your stress level drops.

It is, I'm sure, evident that this is as much about self-preservation as about sensible parenting. The pressure on many mums, who cannot remember their last uninterrupted night's sleep, who feel trapped within the walls of their home and isolated from the outside world yet still have to keep a reasonable house—often with other demanding, energy-sapping pre-schoolers, as well as the baby, to keep amused—is more than many 'captains of industry' ever have to face or could ever comprehend.

Dummies

Dummies are a contentious issue today. As with many other issues, it is a mistake to generalise that they are either 'good' or 'bad'. It is how it is used that can be good or bad, not the dummy itself. Having said that, I must add that there are plenty of babies who don't need a dummy, and to give them out as a matter of course only encourages a dependence that may be entirely unnecessary. But if a baby does not sleep easily, and seems to want to hold on to the bottle (or breast!) when he is tired, a dummy may be just what he's after. In which case, let him have one! (Or at least let him suck it and see.) A dummy used as a comforter in this way can bring immeasurable relief to both parent and child, and should not be dismissed out of hand.

However, a dummy that is used to stop a child crying *during the day* for purposes other than that of aiding sleep is of dubious benefit. Tiny babies cry because they're uncomfortable (too hot, too cold, hungry, wet, dirty, tired or ill), or because they want a cuddle. Older babies and toddlers cry for the same reasons, but also when they are bored or frustrated, or when they have hurt themselves or just want some attention. To use a dummy in these circumstances is to literally make them dumb (albeit temporarily), and may not only become a habit that is extremely difficult to break but also delay or impair the development of speech and thus of understanding. The hidden message in a dummy used indiscriminately to shut a child up is that he himself doesn't really matter, that his feelings, views and wants are of no immediate interest, and that what he does is of little importance *provided he is quiet*. Encouraging dependence on a dummy for short-term gain may well result in long-term embarrassment for the parent and absolute trauma for the child when he has finally to be separated from an object that may have been his support for two, three, or even four years. (At one school I taught in we had occasionally to remind mothers that their children would not be allowed to bring dummies into the nursery class.)

A good rule of thumb is to use a dummy when it comforts your baby and helps him to sleep, but to use it only as a last resort during the day (except, say, before his afternoon nap). Certainly, it helps to have an age in mind by which the dummy should be obsolete—when Abbey was tiny we intended to wean her off it before she was two, but she rejected it herself at about a year and saved us the bother. Our next two babies didn't need one, but if there were to be a surprise number four I would still have a dummy to hand, just in case.

Choose your battles

With a first baby, parents are very much novices in a learning situation, and it's very easy to worry about little things that we wouldn't waste breath or energy over with any subsequent child. Sometimes we're so keen to get it right that we become inflexible, creating a rod for our own backs. For instance, while it is helpful to establish a routine of bathing baby before he goes to bed, it won't have some catastrophic psychological effect if he has occasionally to miss it. Some of us become almost paranoid in our attempts to train our children not to develop a sweet tooth—no sweetened drinks, no chocolate biscuits and certainly no jelly babies! This is probably harder to bear for grandparents, who naturally want to give their grandchildren treats now and again. Others of us can become fanatical about what our babes (and older children) may see and hear on television. All of these things are fine—commendable, even—but should not be allowed to overrule common sense.

It is also easy for some of us to expect too much too soon

from our children as regards instant obedience. I remember becoming terribly frustrated while waiting for my fifteen-month-old to obey my request for her to 'come here'. I sometimes had to wait a rather long time! By the time the second baby reached the same age, I had lightened up sufficiently to realise that it was sometimes more productive either to go and pick her up (if I intended her to come quickly) or to make a game of it by crawling on hands and knees, saying 'I'm coming to get you!', and then enjoy her delighted giggles as I closed in with the clean nappy, or whatever. It is also an enlightening experience to recognise how many times a toddler can be genuinely distracted as she makes her way over the six feet of carpet between her starting-point and the changing mat!

When I first started childminding, the toddler I was looking after was fifteen months old. Although his mum and I had expected the first couple of weeks to be fairly traumatic, he actually settled quite well. He quickly adjusted to life with my two daughters (then aged one and three and a quarter), and when his bottom lip started to tremble he was easily comforted with a cuddle. It really didn't go too badly . . . until the day when I got out the hoover. Luke did not like the hoover. One bit. He screamed, and great tears rolled down his cheeks while his body heaved with sobs. I put the hoover away.

His mum was quite surprised when I told her about it, as he had never particularly objected to *her* hoover. We comforted each other with the thought that it must have been a freak reaction (hope springs eternal in the human breast). But any hope we might have had was quickly superseded by the reality that Luke simply hated my hoover: he seemed terrified of the thing. The choice before me was twofold: either only to hoover when Luke wasn't around (at weekends, or before he arrived or after he had been collected), or to carry on as usual with a view to his becoming used to it. Our joint decision was to persevere until it was no longer a problem for him (or for me). Before I plugged in the monster the next time, I told Luke that I was going to do so, whereupon he burst into tears. So I sat him on a chair with a teddy and his blanket, and got on with it. Abbey and Bekah both had a little turn, and then played with Duplo by his chair while I continued. It was *awful*! I don't know which made the most noise, Luke or the hoover! But I gave him a good cuddle when we had finished, and the howls fairly soon subsided. I determined to hoover that one room each day until it no longer caused a problem for him. It took about a week, and that carpet had never been so immaculate! More importantly, Luke, having overcome his hysteria, was soon wanting to actually help with the job. Hoovering became a lesson in *sharing*, as all three of them took turns to do a little bit. It was quite a relief when that particular enthusiasm wore off and I could get on with the job unhindered.

Children aren't always rational, and it would be very easy sometimes to let their fears and fancies rule our lives. As parents we must decide which potential battles are worth winning, *and for whose sake*, and which little conflicts aren't worth getting stressed about. For me, 'Come, here' to a toddler wasn't worth making a stand for, but hoovering in the hours of daylight was. Other parents will have different priorities, but the important thing is to take time every now and again to step back and assess just what really matters, and why, and what doesn't.

6 From Eighteen Months to Two and a Half

Be in control

No one who has ever lived with small children would deny that they can be exhausting and exasperating in equally strong measure. The good news is that we've all been there—and the *even better news* is that a wealth of experience confirms that, if tiny tantrums are nipped in the bud or if the reasons behind them are understood, many of the worst excesses of toddler behaviour can be avoided. Once you've tuned in to your toddler, the going gets a lot easier! The question is *how* to do it.

Being 'in control' is not actually about controlling your child but, rather, about effectively managing and guiding his behaviour. Very often, it is not so much about punishment as about diverting potential naughtiness before bad habits become established. As already mentioned, with very young children it is possible to deal effectively with problem behaviour by distracting them, by removing them from the situation, or by removing the source of the problem from them. Also, of course, the tone of your voice or the very expression on your face may deter all but the most determined little perishers.

Being in control also means being firm with our children when they deliberately misbehave, and dealing with that unwanted behaviour in such a way as to discourage it from being repeated. If a child does not respond to reasoning—'You must put your coat on because it's cold outside'—the reasoning must be followed up with *appropriate action*. In other words, either the child puts on his coat *or* he stays inside. Don't allow him to catch a chill by finding out for himself how cold it is. This would serve no useful purpose, as a two-year-old would never connect his subsequent chill with his lack of a coat a few days previously. And, predictably, it would have no effect on his future behaviour in the same circumstance. If you have to go out with the child in tow and your judgement is that he needs his coat, the simplest and most effective course of action is to say, 'If you don't put on that coat by the time I've counted to three, Mummy will smack you.'

The first time this happens, the child will probably receive the promised smack before being hustled into the coat, but the next time he will almost certainly put on the hated garment by (or on) the count of three! Coats and colds aside, the real issue here isn't about a battle of wills, but rather about teaching a child obedience. This undoubtedly old-fashioned word, with its even more unfashionable meaning, nevertheless has as much significance and relevance in the relationship between parents and children today as it has ever had. Never has there been an era fraught with more potential dangers for our children; never has there been a time when simple obedience has been more vital. Teaching a child to be obedient and *encouraging* that habit of obedience not only makes life much easier for both parent and child, but it also develops the trust that all children want to have in their parents. Little children usually know exactly what they want (and what they don't want!), but they rarely understand what they *need*; it makes for a much easier childhood if our children respect early the notion that Mummy, or Daddy, knows best.

Set limits

Sooner or later all children will learn that their actions have consequences, and that consequences mean getting adult attention. If we do not give our children enough positive attention (praise, encouragement, interest and physical affection) when they are being good (or kind, or thoughtful, or trying hard), they will try to get our attention by other means. As far as most children are concerned, any attention is better than none. However, as they begin to learn the difference between acceptable and unacceptable behaviour, they need to understand that *all* behaviour has consequences—either nice ones or nasty ones. Setting limits that they can understand is essential, but will only have a positive effect on a child's behaviour if:

- the child understands the agreement, or limit—for instance, 'You can walk if you hold my hand/the buggy.'
- he understands the penalty for breaking the agreement—for instance, 'If you let go you will have to go back into the buggy.'
- the promised penalty is applied, straight away, if the agreement is broken. You may have to bear the child howling all the way home, but next time, he will hold on a lot longer!

Discretion may have a part to play in these little scenarios, and a secondary bargain might be along the lines of:

'Do you want to walk again?'
    'Yes!' (sob, howl!)
'Are you going to hold on this time?'
    'Yes!' (sob, howl!)
'Well, stop that horrible noise and you can have another go!'

But make sure that the racket is at least subsiding, if not completely over, before you let the feet touch the pavement a second time. Secondary bargaining such as this was very effective with my toddlers, but experience has taught me that more than one such second chance, however tempting, is usually counter-productive. Rather a child yelling all the way home than doing the hokey-cokey in and out of the pushchair every ten yards or so. As a general rule, with very young children firm boundaries are much more effective than flexible ones. And *never* use idle threats—'You do that again, and I'll leave you right here in the street!' will have no effect on a child who's heard it a thousand times before.

Some parental pitfalls

One of the most difficult things for parents is to recognise potential 'aggro' situations as they develop and to learn the skills for defusing such time-bombs. Dealing with toddler conflict in an inappropriate way will only intensify the explosion, to the detriment—and exhaustion—of all concerned. Trying to reason a toddler out of a paddy when he is already at the limb-flailing, sob-heaving, glazed-eye stage is just not going to work. The time for reason, or words of any sort, is long since past, and any attempt to talk him out of it is not only doomed to failure but will actually serve to prolong the agony. A 'good smack'—intended perhaps to shock him out of his hysteria rather than punish him for it—is also unlikely to achieve that end, and under such circumstances would probably be delivered a deal harder than the parent would normally deem appropriate (such is the way that stress works on most of us).

The least painful way through a fully developed tantrum is to leave the child to get on with it. If possible, put him into his cot or bedroom and make a cup of tea while the noise (hopefully) subsides. It may be that he will scream himself hoarse before finally falling into an exhausted sleep, or he may slowly expunge his anger and frustration through his heaving sobs until such time as he is willing to be comforted. Distress-

ing and stressful though this waiting process is for all concerned, sitting it out is better by far than wading in with tongue
or temper flying. Often it is not only the child who needs a
chance to calm down. When he eventually relaxes enough to
be comforted or wakes from his exhausted sleep, this is the
time first to cuddle him, to reassure him of your love, and
then to explain gently that it is very naughty to shout and
scream as he did, and to encourage him to say sorry for that
naughtiness. It might also be appropriate to ask him why he
was so cross—it could be that there was a real reason behind
all the histrionics. Understanding that reason is the first step
towards avoiding another similar tantrum. More often than
not, such a young child will be unable to articulate what provoked such temper, even if there *was* a reason. So the burden
lies with the parent to try, with the benefit of hindsight, to
recognise the catalyst or some pattern in the behaviour leading
up to the explosion.

Sometimes a little child 'flips' simply because he wants to
do something himself instead of having it done for him, but
being unable to articulate this he expresses his frustration in
the only way he knows how. It might be something as apparently trivial (to us) as climbing out of his pushchair on his
own, rather than being helped out. It could be that the little
person can *finally* reach the door handle—what a stupendously
exciting achievement *that* is!—and wants to open or shut the
door for himself *and you* in order to practise and perfect his
new skill. While this can be tremendously frustrating for the
time-pressed adult, it is usually quicker and easier in the long
run to humour the child, even to the extent of putting him
back into the pushchair in order for him then to make his own
exit, triumphally unaided. The alternative is to endure the
ensuing heartbroken wailings or tantrum that will actually take
far more time and energy to subdue.

Similarly, when a toddler manages to pick up something he
really shouldn't, especially if he *knows* it's illegal booty, he

will often be somewhat reluctant to relinquish his prize, and 'give that to Mummy' is more likely to harden his grasp than induce him to give it up. If he is not open to bribery and refuses a swap of some sort, try a compromise tactic. Whereas he may not be willing to give up his treasure to you, he may be persuaded to put it back in its rightful home—which is quite useful because it shows you how he managed to get it in the first place—or return it to its rightful owner; or he may be mollified into putting it in a 'safe place' (which you can suggest). Save in exceptional circumstances, forcibly removing the item from the pudgy fist is not usually the wisest course of action; all else having failed, an ultimatum is a more satis-factory way of resolving the conflict than a tug of war. Tell him you are going to count to three, and if he hasn't put the item on the table, or wherever, by the time you reach three, he will get a smack. Most children at this point will tacitly recognise that they are outmanoeuvred, and comply with the superior will-power. If he does, acknowledge it with a suitable comment—'That's better', 'Good boy'; if he doesn't, deliver the promised smack and then remove the object. In the latter case, allow him a little while to cry or sulk, but then encourage him to say sorry and have a cuddle. This might be a good time to explain why he couldn't have that particular thing, emphasising that it wasn't that you wanted to spoil his fun, but that there was a real reason why he couldn't play with it.

My eldest daughter had the worst toddler tantrums of our three girls, partly on account, no doubt, of my inexperience and misunderstanding of her needs. There was one ghastly period when she would quite regularly scream herself into oblivion and eventually wake up with only the barest whisper of a voice left. Sometimes it appeared to be because she was over-tired, yet although she was too miserable and whingey to stay up she fought her afternoon sleep with the same deter-mination, anger and energy with which Frank Bruno attacked Mike Tyson. With much the same final result, too. Although

I didn't understand what set her off in this seeming self-
destruct mode I always knew when it was coming, and despite
my best efforts to head off the outburst I rarely succeeded in
doing so.

One day it happened while we were at my parents' house.
Abbey had asked for a drink and I had offered her orange or
blackcurrant. She chose orange, which surprised me as I knew
she liked blackcurrant and we did not often have it at home.
As the orange was being poured, she decided that she'd really
rather have blackcurrant after all. As I impatiently presented
her with her second choice, she reverted to her first. This
determined indecision—she was quite certain of what she
wanted *until she actually got it*—continued for a few minutes
with both of us becoming more agitated, until eventually I
poured the two drinks into one so as to give her a blackcurrant–
orange mixture. That was it! She shouted and screamed, cried
and stamped and absolutely refused to drink it, still insisting
that she wanted orange—or blackcurrant. Before long she was
completely beyond reason, comfort—or discipline—and the
only course left to me was to manhandle her up to her cot and
let her scream it off. She was still not yet two.

It was some time later that my mother suggested that I was
perhaps not helping Abbey by *offering her a choice*. She really
had wanted orange; she really had wanted blackcurrant; but
because she wanted them equally, she was incapable of choosing one above the other. It made perfect sense—common
sense, even—but I just hadn't seen it. Abbey had always been
very bright, very articulate, very independent—'Abbey do it'
was her response to almost everything. She never wanted help,
she constantly wanted to do things on her own, and for all
these reasons I had decided to encourage that independence
by allowing her to make little decisions about things directly
relating to her (white socks or pink ones, a dress or trousers,
orange or blackcurrant!). It took the common sense of another
mum (mine) to point out to me that *I* was inadvertently causing

By offering her a choice I was perhaps not helping.

Abbey's bad behaviour by offering her choices before she had the cognitive ability to choose one thing over another. The seemingly inevitable and absolutely exhausting tantrums could be painlessly resolved, in this case, by the simple question 'Would you like a drink?'—and by then giving her one of *my* choosing.

Abbey's behaviour improved dramatically after that, because *I* had learnt the lesson that inviting very young children to choose (be it what to eat, what to wear or what to do) is both unnecessary and counter-productive. They have years and years ahead of them in which to take their own decisions, but when they are tiny they need the security of someone making those choices for them. I had also learnt that 'common sense' isn't necessarily that common, and it certainly isn't always that obvious.

The classic toddler tantrum that many parents dread the most is the supermarket shriek. My first two babies never succumbed to this particular vice, so it came as rather a shock when my third, sweet-natured daughter presumed to make up for their deficit. Vulcan infants excepted, children of this age are simply not logical in any way that most adults would recognise. They can shift from beatific contentment to the screaming abdabs and back again, if not in the twinkling of an eye then at least in the space of five minutes. Even when you have seen it happen many times, this sudden eruption followed by complete surrender to diametrically opposed emotions never ceases to amaze.

Bethany was the Jekyll and Hyde case in point. She would start off on our shopping expeditions singing loudly, drawing amused chuckles and coos from passers-by, and seeming the epitome of contented toddlerhood. Then we would pass through the doors of the supermarket and the mood would start to change. Our rule was that she either held on to the trolley or she sat in it. The trouble would usually start because she wanted to hold my hand instead of the trolley. Only someone who has ever attempted to steer a loaded trolley single-handed would appreciate the sheer impracticality of her desire. Sometimes she would be placated for a while by helping to push the trolley, but often that would evolve in her mind into a wish to push the trolley alone, and she would try to remove my hands from the handle. She might be distracted for a while by being allowed to hold one of the groceries (not the eggs), but inevitably it got to the point where she wanted to choose the item she was to carry. Most of her choices were not practical: they might be chewable (ham, cheese), bruisable (fruit, veg), splittable when dropped (bags of dried fruit, sugar, flour), too big (loo rolls, cornflakes), too heavy (washing powder, squash), too openable (margarine, yoghurt), and so forth.

All this time the whingeing would be escalating, as would the lapses from holding on to the trolley. Eventually she would be hoiked, kicking and screaming, into the seat intended for such little people. The screaming would then continue all the way round the shop, back to the carpark, and often till we arrived home. Speaking extremely firmly to her had an impact for as long as I kept up eye contact, but the moment I looked away to continue the shopping, she would be off again. Smacking her under such circumstances would only have increased the noise level and both our discomfort (her rage and my embarrassment!), and shouting at her would merely have indicated a loss of self-control on my part.

On these uncomfortable occasions, once the tantrum was under way there was little I could do but try to ignore it and finish the shopping as swiftly as possible. When we arrived home, if the tantrum had passed I would tell Bethany that she had been very naughty for making such a dreadful noise, and that she should say sorry for doing so. This she did on all but one occasion, and we were able to put the incident behind us (until the next time!).

If she hadn't stopped the yelling by the time we got home, or if she refused to say sorry, I would put her in her cot, telling her she could come out when she had stopped the noise. Had I done this with my older two girls at the same age (two and a half), they would have quickly stopped the bawling in order to come downstairs again. But not Bethany! She cried all the louder and only stopped when I went up to her five minutes later. Then I was able to say, 'Have you stopped that dreadful noise yet?' ('Ye-e-e-es Mummy'), 'Are you ready to say sorry now?' ('Sorry, Mummy'). And that would be that. If she *wasn't* ready, I would leave her again for a further five minutes. It never needed more than that. But facing up to and apologising for her naughtiness in this way didn't actually affect her behaviour the next time we went shopping. The trolley tantrum was becoming a habit. As soon as she saw the trolley she would immediately begin to get into grizzle mode, even if she'd been perfectly happy the second before.

Any sort of naughtiness can become a habit if it is not dealt with effectively early on, and this was one habit I needed to break before it became too entrenched. Clearly, the trolley was the trigger; Bethany wanted to do what I did—namely, walk freely around the shop, picking up bits and pieces as I do so. Equally clearly, I could not dispense with the trolley, and she could not be allowed to wander off every time she'd had enough of holding on.

Solution? Change the rules, since the current set weren't working. Instead of giving her the option of being a good girl and holding on, she would have to sit in the hated trolley seat from the word go, despite her protests. Once she realised that it was a *fait accompli* with no alternative options, she would have to accept it. Before beginning this new regime I explained to my tiny daughter that she would have to sit in the trolley, so that it wouldn't come as too much of a shock. Nevertheless, her howls of protest thoroughly embarrassed me all round the shop, and beyond. The next time we went to the supermarket it was the same. The third time she howled only up to half-way round. The fourth time she made a token protest as I lifted her in, and thereafter she accepted that she was going to ride in the trolley and that was that. My embarrassment had been a small price to pay in exchange for the knowledge that I could expect a well behaved little girl on *most* future shopping-trolley days.

When your child is screaming his head off in public and there is nothing you can do about it, the key to coping is to try to stay calm yourself and remember that most bystanders who have ever had children will have experienced the same nightmare. Later on, when everything has calmed down, you may be able to identify a reason for his behaviour, and work out a possible strategy for dealing with it on future occasions. If there really is no obvious way of approaching the problem, don't despair. It's just a particularly difficult stage your child is going through . . . and it *will* pass. Try to concentrate on, and praise, his good behaviour at other times, rather than continually focusing on his misdeed, and above all make sure that he has more of your attention, time and energy when he is not being naughty than when he is.

Her howls of protest thoroughly embarrassed me all round the shop.

If a child is continuously naughty for no apparent reason, there's a good chance he's doing it for the attention it brings him. As parents, we then need to ask ourselves seriously why he is so desperate for our attention. How much time have we given him today? When was the last time we read him a story, did a puzzle together, played with the Duplo, chased him round the garden, played hide and seek? When was the last time we held his hand, gave him a cuddle or kissed him better (from wounds real or imagined)? When was the last time we said 'Well done!' 'What a clever boy', 'That was a kind thing to do', 'I love you'? There are times for all of us when the answers to these questions will tell us all we need to know.

Communicating

Giving time to our children, communicating meaningfully with them on *their* level, doesn't have to be hard work or brain-deadening; on the contrary, it can be—should be—great fun.

Children are great lovers of fun: innocent slapstick, funny faces, silly voices. They especially love the familiarity of special words and pet names, and far from limiting or restricting their language development these may encourage little people to experiment more with words and sounds. This kind of 'baby talk' is wrongly disparaged, often by those who have no ongoing day-to-day experience of very young children. Never be embarrassed to extend your vocabulary to such words and phrases as 'scrummy, yummy in your tummy', 'easy-peasy lemon squeezy', 'quished and quashed'—this last is far more descriptive and demonstrable than 'run over' or 'flattened'. My youngest daughter is very partial to 'jilly jolly jelly' which she now calls 'jilly jolly', and she has a special word for her blanket—'bankti'—which my middle daughter has adopted too (but only for use at home). It's a special language just for us; it has an unspoken familiarity and friendliness about it that we all treasure while it lasts, for we know that the time will come all too quickly when 'our baby' will use the same vocabulary as everyone else, and we shall have to struggle to remember those special baby words.

Not everybody feels comfortable talking about tum-tums and toe-toes, fingles (fingers!) and feeties, but the important thing at this age is not *how* we say things, but *that* we say them. Some parents may be concerned that their baby's verbal development might be delayed by experimental or alliterative baby-talk. Others may worry that descriptive language of the 'moo-cow', 'baa-lamb' variety indicates a lack of awareness of their child's ability to understand or use proper words. They fear that such apparently low expectations on their part might limit or restrict their child's cognitive skills and ability to communicate.

My view is that 'creative' nouns like 'moo-cow' can give the child additional information about the animal and, by adding the dimension of sound, make it more interesting and therefore easier to distinguish from other animals. My *experi-*

ence is that, however often I may have enthused over 'baby baa-lambs' and such like, most children naturally drop the babyism as they reach school age.

Rather than worrying about using a proper noun or correct adjective, my personal concern with regard to language development in young children is more that they should learn the use of properly constructed sentences—'Do you want (to do) a wee-wee?' as opposed to 'Wanna wee?'—and that they should be encouraged to say 'Can I do it please?' rather than 'Me do it'.

I would also distinguish between baby *talk* and baby *voices*. Even two-year-olds can affect a baby tone—usually when they are trying to get away with not doing as they are told! This is something to discourage before it becomes a habit, not least because it's jolly irritating!

The bottom line is, if baby-talk comes naturally to you, use it and enjoy it while you can—your child may grow out of it before you do!

The importance of talking with (not at) our children cannot be overstated, and implied in this is listening to them as well. Children (even tinies) also love rhyming words, rhythm and alliteration; all these devices help bring language to life as well as making instructions more fun—'Take those fiddle-fingers away from that cake', 'Stop worming and squirming while I'm washing your face!'

This is also the age at which to start gently insisting on 'please' and 'thank you'. It does help, of course, if the words are already familiar because Mummy and Daddy use them! When your precious child demands a drink in typical two-year-old style—'Want more drink, Daddy,' or (the even more imperative) 'Need more drink!'), say 'Can I have another drink, *please*?' for him to repeat. He will probably mumble the first bit in his haste to achieve the object of his heart's desire, but you should get a clear 'please' (or 'pease', anyway) at the end of it. And as you hand him the promised refill, hang on to it until he has said what passes for 'Thank you'. Again, you will probably have to remind him for the first few hundred times, but such is life.

Another good habit which even toddlers can learn is putting their hands to their mouths when they cough. Learning from example, plus a touch of amateur dramatics on the part of the parent, is a winning formula. A little bit of over-acting from the adult with the genuine (or feigned) cough, complemented with lots of enthusiasm for the child with the real (or feigned) cough when he mimes the desired action, may not win any Oscars, but it will help the message home. With any 'good manners', it is important to remember that all children will need patient reminding before the habit becomes automatic, and that the best way to encourage them is to notice and praise them when they do do it without being prompted.

Potty-training

Most parents think about potty-training when their child is this age, and for some it can be a real problem. The best way to approach the process is to be as laid-back and as practical about it as you can. The last thing to worry about is what everyone else's toddlers are doing.

The first thing to take into account may be the time of year. It is much easier to deal with the 'accidents' and washing when the days are warm and sunny, and much more comfortable for the child to wander around half-naked when it's 70 degrees in the shade. Potty-training in winter just because he has reached a certain age, rather than because he seems ready for it, has always seemed to me an unnatural preoccupation. However, if your child is ready to use the potty when the snow is lying thick on the ground, by all means go for it! As in everything else, children are 'ready' to start potting at different ages and some will take longer than others. If, for instance, your child is approaching two but, when you've tried to introduce him to the potty, doesn't seem to have a clue about using it, put it away for a few weeks and then have another go. I tried to potty-train my first daughter a month before her second birthday. As the results were rather more miss than hit, and I was six months pregnant at the time, I decided after a week that it wasn't worth the hassle and I put the potty away. Three weeks later we had another go. This time something just clicked, and Abbey was clean and dry within two weeks. Of course we still had a few interesting incidents, such as when Abbey, busy in the garden, realised she wasn't going to make it to the potty in time, so squatted down and delivered herself of the most enormous poo, then promptly picked it up, carried it into the kitchen and proudly offered it to me. Arggh!

Although some mums successfully potty-train their babies before they reach their first birthday, my youngest daughter was over two and a half before the weather was right! Even then, for a couple of weeks we were beginning to wonder whether there was any connection at all between her brain and her bladder! The garden path had little wet patches all over it, but the potty remained conspicuously dry. We rapidly ran out of 'knick-knocks' despite the glorious sunshine, and allowed her birthday suit several all-day airings. Then one day came the glorious shout from one of her sisters, 'Bethany's done a wee-wee in the potty!' It still took several weeks after that before she was reliably dry, and even longer before she was reliably clean. Such was the excitement at the first poo in the potty that we all had to admire it (loudly and at length) before eventually I was permitted to tip it into the loo. Then the proud pooper proceeded to blow kisses fondly after it as it 'went for a swim', and for weeks after insisted on waving bye-bye to the contents of every potty.

From nappy to knick-knocks seemed to take for ever in Bethany's case, but was actually only about six weeks. It did seem a long time and, particularly during the first few weeks, we would sometimes have a day off to give us both a break.

However, when I could count on her remaining dry during the day I left off her nappy for her afternoon sleep with relatively few 'accidents', and was pleased to discover that once she knew what she was doing she actually had very good bladder control.

The last challenge is always that of leaving off the nappy at night, and there are various strategies to help with this. The first is to invest in a mattress protector if you haven't already got one! An old plastic table-cloth will do, but these can be a bit sweaty, especially in hot weather, so it's advisable to use a towel between the plastic cloth and the sheet for comfort's sake. Some parents start nappyless nights by refusing any drinks after a specific time in the afternoon or early evening. I have never done this as my girls have always had a bedtime drink, but all the same it is only common sense to monitor and restrict, if necessary, what the child drinks after five o'clock or so (assuming he will be going to bed sometime between six and eight o'clock).

In addition to reminding him to do a wee last thing before he gets into bed, many parents pot their child when they themselves go to bed. This is usually a successful move, but can become counter-productive if it continues too long: the child may come to rely more on being potted than on heeding the messages from his own bladder. When my children first slept without a nappy, I told them to call me (or knock on the wall) if they needed a wee in the night. It's a lot to expect a little one to wake up in time *and* get to the potty or loo in near-darkness and not make a mess somewhere. Trainer-pants (plastic with a towelling lining) also proved invaluable, and they are well worth the investment. Often the child will lose a drop of wee before he fully wakes, but the trainer-pants will catch this and save the palaver of changing the sheet in the middle of the night. (It's much easier to change the pants than change the bed.) Even when a child is regularly dry at night, there may still be the occasional accident, up to school age and beyond. If this doesn't happen to your child, count your bless-ings; if it does, deal with it with as little fuss as possible—it's bad enough for the child being up in the middle of the night without him being upset as well. If you show your frustration at yet *another* wet bed, the effect on your child will probably be to make him more anxious about it, which will have the oppo-site effect to what was intended. A child should never be made to feel guilty or naughty for doing something over which he has no control. Crossness from the parent for something that he cannot help will only distress him—and make a return to sleep more difficult for him and you.

If a child suddenly starts to wet the bed when previously he has been dry, the reason will either be that he is a little 'off-colour' and about to go down with something, or that he is feeling stressed. Problems within the family or a sudden change in circumstances (such as moving house) can cause a little one great insecurity. Unable to understand or articulate his confusion, bedwetting may be the only obvious indicator that he is significantly upset by changes around him. In such cases it is even more important to remain calm and be gentle with a bedwetter and, understanding the 'sign', to try to work out some way of 'undoing' the anguish your child is feeling.

Perhaps the most fundamental strategy for house-training children is a combination of patience and humour, together with a willingness to accept that accidents can, do, and will happen.

Happy, smiling faces

Little children don't need a great deal of money spent on them to keep them happy and stimulated. What they do need is our time and interest. There are lots of things that toddlers will start to enjoy that six months previously they would have had no interest in. This is the time to re-acquaint yourself with long-forgotten nursery rhymes and maybe learn some new ones, and certainly invest in one or more of the nursery tapes specifically aimed at this age group. Young children love the familiarity of repetition, and listening to a well loved tape has taught my children more rhymes and songs than I could ever have remembered. Singing along with (or without) the music also gives some children great pleasure, and can serve as a distraction and comfort after little upsets. Visiting the children's library can almost be a trial—there are so many beautifully illustrated books to choose from. Children of this age derive great pleasure from the pictures and simply told stories, especially if a loved adult is enjoying the story with them. Before they can enjoy books on their own, they need to experience the wonder of books through the enthusiasm of someone they love. It's a great thing for children to be familiar with books—and how to treat them—from a young age; and while some may be too expensive to buy, there's no shortage at any children's library.

There are some wonderful toys on the market for all ages, but it's often the simplest things that give the greatest pleasure to very young children. All of mine developed a fascination for screw-top lids, and would play for ages with empty plastic bottles, screwing the lid on, taking it off again, stuffing things inside the bottle, finding out if it would shake or rattle (and getting frustrated when things got stuck!). These were also hugely interesting to play with in the bath or paddling-pool. They enjoyed playing with pegs, tipping them all over the floor, clipping them on to each other and sorting them into heaps. My first daughter took great delight in noisily ripping paper (newspaper, paper bags, computer paper) and then stuffing the shreds into the bin. I think she enjoyed her ability to make a huge mess and get rid of it again in equal measure to the sound and power in the action of tearing. Favourite garden toys have always been anything that could be used to dig with (spade, trowel, fork, stick), especially when combined with a bucket or bowl and an illegal water 'find'. 'We're making medicine,' one two-year-old gleefully informed me as he and my daughter stirred a concoction of rainwater, earth, grass and dandelion heads. I instantly resolved never to be ill again.

Word games are great fun for children, and convenient for adults because they don't involve any mess, require no props, and can be played any time, anywhere, *and* when everyday tasks are being done. My children all loved 'Where's Daddy?':

'Is he at home?'
  'No!'
'Is he at school?'
  'No!'
'Is he in the garden?'
  'No!'
'Is he up the chimney?'
  'No!'
'Is he at work?'
  '*Yes!*'

Another of my children's favourites was 'What does doggy/pussy/sheep/cow/duck/owl/fish say?' '*Woof woof!*' (and so on).

There are many variations on this sort of theme that are likely to be greeted with 'Do it again, Mummy!' time after time. Despite the repetition, it doesn't have to become boring for the adult. The possibilities are endless: 'What does Daddy say?'—'What's for dinner?'; 'What does Mummy say?'—'I need some chocolate!'

Counting things (stairs, cars, fingers, buttons) comes into its own at this age, and can be backed up with all the nursery rhymes, songs and stories that feature numbers. Similarly, colours can be learnt through the use of 'Bring me . . .' and 'Show me . . .' games—'Bring me a red brick!', 'Show me a blue car!'. This is a fun and easy way for any child to learn. The only 'rules' are (1) don't push it if the child has had enough, and (2) don't get cross when young Einstein gets it wrong! If he is confidently calling every colour *red*, single out one other colour and concentrate on that: for instance, 'You make a red tower with those bricks, and I'll make a yellow tower with these.'

Playing with our children in this way is *so* important, not only because we are giving them our time and attention, and giving their toys and activities value and respect in *their eyes* because of *our interest*, nor even mainly because of the learning that can take place through our interaction with them. Arguably the greatest significance of playing with our children is that *it teaches them how to play*. Children can't know the fun that can be had from a box of Duplo unless someone shows them—they learn from the experience of observation and participation. Their imagination is all there, but it may remain hidden, unused and undeveloped unless someone stimulates and encourages them to take it out and try it out. Toddlers (and older children) whose parents share in their games will be far more able and content to play on their own, and for much longer, than a child who has never been played with.

Of course, there are times when our children don't want our input, either because they're in a wonderful make-believe world of their own which needs no adult contribution, or because they're doing something they shouldn't! The latter is usually indicated by a strange calm, and the moral of that is, always pay *instant* attention to unusual silences!

7   From Two and a Half to Three and a Half

Be firm but fair

This is a really exciting age for a child to be. Both his understanding and his vocabulary are developing. There are more and more things that he can do and that he'd like to try—his whole world is full of exploration and discovery. It's a lovely stage for a parent to watch, too, seeing not only the independence and abilities of her 'baby' multiply, but also being aware of his developing character and personality. There is the down side, though, as anyone who has experienced the 'Why?' offensive will testify!

Increasing yet sometimes misplaced confidence in a three-year-old will often result in an increase in potential conflict situations as and when the nearly irrepressible child meets the usually immovable force, the No word. Being reasonable when your child is determinedly *un*reasonable can take great self-control, will-power and energy, and sometimes it is appropriate to use the time-honoured 'Because I say so' when you have exhausted every logical and rational argument as to why, for example, you can't keep an elephant in the back garden. There may be times however, when it is pertinent to use this particular device rather earlier in the confrontation, simply to emphasise that the balance of power between parent and child is not equal, any more than is the balance of experience or responsibility. Children do need to learn that enough is enough, and in some situations they need to be made aware of it sooner than in others.

That said, more often than not it is far better, and more rewarding, to explain to a child of this age why you have said no. Sometimes it may be appropriate to get him to explain to you why he can't do a certain thing:

> 'Mummy, can I play in the garden?'
> 'Not now, sweetheart.'
> *'Why?'*
> 'Why do you think? You tell me.'
> 'Because it's bedtime.'
> 'Yes—anything else?'
> 'Cos it's too cold.'
> 'Mmmmmmmm, anything else?'
> 'It's raining . . . and all dark.'
> 'Mmmm . . .'
> 'And cos I'm in bed!'
> 'What a lot of reasons! You can play in the garden tomorrow. Night-night!'

Yet there may be times when your child's reasoning persuades you to change your mind, or makes you realise that you were wrong about something. Concede defeat graciously and commend the child for sticking to his guns. Make sure he understands that you have changed your mind due to his reasoning, not simply to stop him nagging. If it is appropriate, apologise for having misunderstood or not listened properly earlier on. Then enjoy with him the satisfaction and pride that your respect has given him.

Sometimes we need to be reasonable with ourselves, accept that we are not perfect, that we won't always do *or know* the right or best thing in every situation. This does not mean we are failures as parents. In any case, what a terrible burden it would be for any child to have a perfect parent—what an impossible example to live up to. The important thing for us, as for our children, is to do our best.

Be realistic

Part of being realistic as parents is being able to recognise when apparent naughtiness isn't actually any such thing. It helps to remember that children are not mini-adults. They are not responsible for what they do in the same way as adults are, and so allowances must be made for:

- clumsiness, accidents;
- forgetfulness;
- not understanding, misunderstanding;
- not listening, not concentrating, not trying;
- being tired;
- inability to do or understand something;
- getting it wrong;
- wanting attention.

All of these call for a response of some sort, but punishment isn't the right one. Pure childishness alone can never be a justification for punishment. This does not mean that we should allow our children to become careless—if they break or spill something, get them to help clear away the mess, or even to do it on their own if they are capable of doing so. As parents we need to distinguish between when our children are deliberately naughty and when they are simply being children. We also need to encourage them always to *tell us* if something has been spilled or broken, and to do so *straight away*, not half an hour after the event. It is possible that, by so doing, a greater mess can be avoided, further damage prevented and the original breakage mended, salvaged or restored. Frustrating though it is to have to clear up the mess and repot the busy lizzie because some little person got over-excited looping the loop in his aeroplane, it's much easier to do it *before* it's been trodden all over the house. 'Thank you for telling me' goes a long way towards reassuring the child that he did the right thing in confessing to his crash landing.

Sometimes apparent naughtiness can occur because we as parents haven't made it clear what the boundaries are, or explained the right way to behave in a new situation. The child who happily picks the heads off your prize tulips and pulls them to pieces all over the garden isn't being naughty if he has never been told not to pick the flowers. Similarly, the three-year-old who scribbles all over the wallpaper is not really at fault if he has never learnt that the only place to draw is on the table or floor with the paper that Mummy provides for that purpose. If your child appears predisposed to such avant-garde artistry, it's a sensible precaution to keep all drawing materials out of temptation's way. It's no hardship or humiliation for him to have to ask for his pencils and learn to return them when he has finished, and this also makes his creative endeavours much easier to monitor. It is often easier to have more rules rather than fewer: there is great security and safety for the child who knows exactly what he can and can't do, and peace of mind for the parent, too.

It's not only what little children do that can be mistakenly perceived as naughtiness, but also what they say and how they say it. They often say things that are funny, usually because they've used completely the wrong word or because they're mimicking something an adult has said and it sounds incongruous. There are lots of occasions when they see laughter as approval and encouragement but *without understanding why*. As a result, there are other, less happy, occasions when they may try to repeat a previous success only to find, much to their bewilderment, that they are met with embarrassment, disapproval or even anger. Similarly, there are certain things that may be natural for a child to talk about or comment on in the home, with his immediate family, but which are inappropriate anywhere else. Many parents will have experienced the colour-changing embarrassment of a small child in a public lavatory, his clear, piping voice magnified by the acoustics of that echoing chamber. 'Daddy, why is that man so fat?' or 'Mummy, are you going to do a poo?' Or, even worse, 'I think that lady has done a big one—I can smell it.' Ohhh dear!

Many toddlers go through a 'No!' phase, when they start to say the word with real passion, commitment and volume, regardless of what you may be asking them. They seem suddenly to understand and enjoy the *power* and completeness of the word, without having yet realised that it isn't always appropriate or necessary. The first time this loud negative comes hurtling through the air with almost machine-gun rapidity it's rather a shock to the system, but it can also be impossible not to laugh at:

'Look at the rain outside, Bekah!'
  '*No!*'
'Oh! Are you too busy?'
  '*No!*'
'Can you hear it then?'
  '*No!*'
'Shall we have some tea—'
  '*No!*'
'—and a piece of cake?'
  '*No!*'
'A chocolate biscuit, then?'
  '*Nooooyes!*'

But what may be funny in one situation isn't necessarily so in another, and a child may become very confused by the inconsistency, as he perceives it, of the adult response to his behaviour. As parents we sometimes need to recognise this, and realise that the little comedian isn't actually being as defiant or cheeky as would at first appear. He's just going for the encore from the previous day's entertainment. This doesn't mean that his behaviour should go unchecked, though. When a child is older, you can explain why it isn't funny any more, but with children this young it's not always possible to do so. Sometimes the best solution is to ignore the behaviour (especially if it's an unwanted word he's picked up). Making a song and dance about it would simply draw attention to it and make it more difficult to forget. It may be appropriate to firmly say no to him, or to somehow distract him. When Bethany was going through her 'No!' phase, every time she said it I responded with 'No *thank* you!' After a while she started to copy the new version, complete with exaggerated inflection.

A very practical consideration that is not always recognised is that small children have a very different vantage point from adults—about three feet lower!—and they often cannot see everything that we can. It can sometimes save upsets and misunderstandings to bend down and get a child's eye view of a situation. The difference between their view and ours can be quite surprising. Equally, we usually 'talk down' to them from our lofty adult height, but it's important sometimes to get on a level with them—either by bringing them up to our stratosphere or by bending down to theirs!

Such eyeball-to-eyeball communication demonstrates unmistakably that they have our whole attention, and expresses a solidarity and interest on our part that can be difficult to achieve from a vertical gap of three feet or more. This is especially important when explaining something to a child—when you may need to read from his face whether he really understands what you are saying—or when he is explaining something to you. Being 'on the level' with a child also makes it easier to catch—and keep—eye contact, which is particularly important when, in a situation where he may have been naughty, you want him to feel secure enough to tell you the truth. In such a case it helps to talk softly and slowly, maybe with your arm around him or holding his hands. The calm and caring presence and touch of an adult will reassure a little

Small children have a very different vantage point from adults.

person that it will be OK no matter what terrible misdeed he has committed! In any case, being angry or shouting at him will do nothing to encourage him to tell the truth, and may make him more wary, not of repeating his mistake, but of being found out.

Be wise: into the mouths of babes and sucklings

Little children do not always know, or *remember*, what to say in every situation— 'Please' and 'Thank you' are the obvious examples! Sometimes it is fitting to help them out by telling them the 'right' thing to say. In learning-to-share situations where two children both want to use the one pair of scissors or to ride the red tricycle, it can make a surprising difference to teach them 'Please may I have that when you've finished?', or even 'Is it my turn yet?' It would of course, be a much easier option to buy a second pair of scissors or a matching red trike, and that would solve the problem in the short term.

(So would putting the scissors away or banning the bike.) However, that would not even begin to tackle the main difficulty, which has nothing to do with scissors or trikes and everything to do with *sharing*. The word 'share' represents far too abstract a concept for little children to understand, but what they can learn from is the practical reality of *taking turns*. When they were younger, my children and their cousins used to have great fun taking turns jumping off Grandma's pouffe! At home, they used to take turns jumping down the stairs— on the understanding that they mustn't leap from higher than the fourth step, and that if they hurt themselves they would get scant sympathy! There are safer ways of taking turns, but they are often not half so much fun!

When a squabble is brewing, suggest to the child that he say 'Can I have it in a minute, please?' (as opposed to 'I want it' or 'It's *mine*!'). The difference the right words can make is quite significant. Equally, the best way of winkling out the truth is not 'Who did that?' but 'How did that happen?' The child may then need encouragement to say 'I'm sorry, Mummy, it was me' or 'I did, but it was an accident.' Say it for him, and let him copy your words. If the 'accident' involved hurting someone else, then he must say sorry to the injured party—or his incomplete comprehension of logic might tell him that it's OK to hurt someone if you do so in a genuine accident! When a child has owned up to being the cause of some mishap, reward his honesty with a cuddle and 'Thank you for telling me, darling—now, help me clear it up' or 'You won't do it again, will you?' Sometimes the right words might be 'I'm sorry, I won't do it again' or the more realistic 'I'll *try* not to do it again.'

Words are tremendously powerful. Used sensitively to correct, comfort and encourage, the right ones can help along the right attitude, too.

A common 'sticky' situation with pre-schoolers occurs when they have to leave an activity or place in which they've been having fun. An effective way of dealing with this is to give the child warning that he'll soon have to stop or to leave— 'We'll have to go in a minute/get ready to say goodbye/have one last turn, OK?'; or 'You've got five minutes before we have to start tidying up, all right?' It can be helpful to count down the minutes as the time passes, as this not only keeps the child's attention on the fact of the imminent departure but also encourages an awareness of how long a minute, or five, is. Whatever the strategy, always get a response from him, otherwise he may later claim that he didn't hear you. Parents have to be crafty, too! Parents also have to be fair, however, and it isn't reasonable to give a child instructions to get ready to go and then proceed to chat with his friend's mother for a further half-hour!

When this approach doesn't work, something more tangible is called for. This could be anything from the promise (or provision) of a sweet to the promise (or delivery) of a smack! While the former can have its uses, it is clearly not a good idea to *regularly* reward defiance with bribery! Trying to elicit good behaviour in this way can actually result in reinforcing the initial disobedience; you may be training the child to become manipulative and devious, by apparently *rewarding* his naughty behaviour.

Given the circumstances, the old faithful of repeating the instruction and counting to three before following through with 'Well done!' or a smack, as appropriate, is probably the most effective action you can now take. If the child is *still* unwilling to leave, then you have no option but to impose your superior size, strength and power to physically remove him from the scene (and straight away—not after a protracted bout of bargaining). This is not an abuse of your child's rights, feelings or physical integrity, but simply one of life's lessons that has to be learnt.

Least helpful in this situation is for the parent, despite the conciseness of her initial instruction, to allow herself to be drawn into a pleading or reasoning dialogue with her defiant offspring. I once watched a mother try to entice her middle child into the car after a family visit. His siblings were already belted up and ready to go, but had to wait for fully twenty minutes while the harassed and clearly embarrassed mother pandered to the attention-seeking of the rebel. She tried first to cajole, then reason, then joke him into obedience. The child was clearly enjoying the confrontation and revelling in the fact that he was so obviously in control. When the mother reluctantly threatened a smack, he smirked at her in a way that revealed quite unambiguously that he didn't believe she would deliver. There followed a chase around a parked car before he was caught and tapped ever so lightly on the leg. At this he contemptuously broke free and the chase around the car began again. This time he was caught firmly and bundled, still insolently uncooperative, into the car.

That child had thoroughly enjoyed wielding his power over his mother, and had exploited her ineffectualness to the detriment of all concerned. At the end of the performance he received no meaningful penalty for his disobedience and thus no disincentive to repeating the behaviour. The pained telling off he had received was clearly water off a duck's back, and one could not help but ponder on how much more the mother could take. What was clear was that the child was crying out for some firm rules and more effective behaviour management.

Wait till your father gets home!

This much derided idea can still have a very positive place in the training of our children, if the original concept is turned around. Far from being a threat signalling rejection and anger when Daddy arrives, it can be the very opposite: a reward promising excitement and approval from the other most important person in the young child's life. When he does or says or sees something special, what significance that thing is given and what positive reinforcement, if it's important enough to show or tell Daddy about. Of course, a three-year-old will probably not remember the incident without prompting (and Daddy may need help in interpreting his child's enthusiasm!), but having something good to share at the end of the day is a great habit to get into. Daddy's interest and pleasure in whatever little experience or achievement is on offer will be a great inducement to want to be good, kind, clever or whatever on future days too. An extra plus is that this can also be a real aid to the development of memory: remembering something that will bring the reward of attention and praise is a good incentive for making those little grey cells do a bit of over-time.

Food, glorious food

Some children just love food and appear to be constantly thinking of the next meal. Others struggle to finish whatever is put before them, and still others develop very definite ideas of what they will and won't eat. But while it is possible that a child will overeat to the point of making himself sick, a normal child will not naturally starve, despite an appearance of eating enough only to keep a sparrow alive. Worrying about the *quantity* of food a child eats is a waste of energy, unless he is actually losing weight, in which case take him to the doctor. That aside, if your child is a poor eater, try to concentrate on the *quality* of what he is eating, and don't let him fill up between meals on crisps and sweets or sweet drinks. If he eats little, but continually wants to drink, give him plain water after the first beaker of squash or juice. If he has become used to having squash on tap, he won't like it . . . and if he isn't genuinely thirsty, he won't drink it, either! (If he continues to drink an unusual amount of water, take him to the doctor. Abnormal thirst can be a sign of diabetes.)

Drinking can become a comfort habit for some children, particularly if they are still using a bottle. With most children who guzzle too much—who drink not because they are thirsty but because they love the sweetness of their tipple—extra dilution of squashes will help diminish their desire for excess drinks. One child I knew used to down a two-litre bottle of squash during an hour's trip to the shops. It cost his mother a fortune not only in squash but also in nappies, and so filled his tummy that he didn't eat properly and appeared anaemic and pale. Having had him checked out by the doctor, who discovered no medical problem, she then had to face the difficult task of weaning him off the squash, which she had inadvertently allowed to become his 'comforter'.

Some little children simply haven't attuned their tummies to the same eating patterns as the rest of us: breakfast with their older siblings before they go to school may be just that little bit too early, whereas eating on the return from school may make all the difference. Most children enjoy a snack at mid-morning, and many will prefer a few raisins or a couple of dates to a biscuit, given the choice. Fresh fruit is another alternative.

The general eating rules that have worked in our house are:

- First course before pudding! In order to get pudding, at least some of the first course must be consumed, if not all. This is a generously flexible rule, designed to accommodate the age and appetite of each individual child.
- No one has seconds of pudding if they haven't eaten *all* their first course!
- All are encouraged to eat a little of everything, including the things they don't like. Children who are allowed to leave anything they are not keen on often become faddy and finicky eaters, sometimes reaching the stage where they will not try anything new and becoming increasingly restrictive in what they *will* eat. If they are encouraged to eat the

things they don't like first, thus saving the best till last, most children will respond positively—provided they are not given half a plateful of the hated parsnips, liver or Brussels sprouts!

A difficulty for some parents is remembering not to say in front of a child, 'Oh, he won't like that.' Children who hear that they won't like something, especially if it's green, are apt to believe it! And if they're not *expected* to eat it, they often won't even try it. Some parents have so capitulated to the restricted tastes of their children that, rather than risk further waste or refusals, if something unfamiliar is offered they will speak *for* their children, saying 'No thank you, they won't eat that.' This acceptance of the unfortunate status quo will do nothing to improve the situation.

For those children who are genuinely not that interested in food the best plan is to give them the same as everybody else but in *much* smaller quantities. A tiny dinner set in the middle of a plate will appear much more manageable to a small eater than a 'healthy'-sized portion, even given the understanding that it doesn't all have to be eaten.

A pet theory of mine is that children are inclined to eat better if they do so regularly with their parents (or other adults) as well as with other children. Certainly, eating in company is better than eating alone, no matter how big or little you may be. Seeing a parent enjoying a meal and finishing up her plateful has to be a good example to little people, and the prospect of pudding to come can be an added incentive to eat up. Sometimes pudding can not only be used as an inducement to eat the preceding course, but can also be effectively withheld as a check to bad behaviour at the table. I heard of one child whose parents regularly employed this tactic, but apparently he was so badly behaved that he hadn't had pudding for weeks. Clearly, the check wasn't working, so it was high time to try something else.

I also believe that it is important for a child to expect to eat at the table, rather than having a tray or plate on his lap. Eating in front of the television is a habit to discourage, on the grounds that it fosters laziness and neglects the discipline of using the 'off' switch. The enjoyment and appreciation of food should be complemented by company and conversation, not compromised by the flickering screen in the corner of the room.

Things to do

From about the age of two, many children will begin to take an interest in children's TV programmes such as 'Playbus', 'Sesame Street' and some of the earlier 'children's hour' items. Their enjoyment and understanding will be greatly enhanced if they can watch with an adult and chat about what they see, maybe relating it to their own experience. I often do a bit of ironing when 'Playbus' is on, and it is noticeable that Bethany, at almost three, watches far more avidly when I'm there with her than when I'm not. For most three-year-olds a whole hour of 'Sesame Street' is too long for sustained concentration, but it can be useful as an occasional 'baby-sitter', to enable the weary parent to get on with some essential task without being interrupted every three minutes. I'm not advocating using the TV habitually in this way, but it can have its advantages.

One rule we have always insisted on is that our children never turn the TV on without asking first, and when the programme they are watching is over, they switch it off again. This imbues in them a respect for the TV; an understanding that it is not a toy, but a tool to be used in a certain—selective—way. It also forges an acceptance from the very earliest days that not all programmes are appropriate for children, and puts the onus of choice squarely on the parent.

Popular activities for this age group will of course vary from child to child, but I don't think the child has yet been born who doesn't enjoy play-dough. The home-made offering does not last as well as the commercial variety, Playdoh, but this point is nullified by its other advantages—it's quick, easy and very cheap to make:

1 cup of plain flour
½ cup of salt
1 cup of coloured water (use food colourings)
1–1½ tablespoons of cooking oil
2 teaspoons of cream of tartar (vital ingredient—play-dough remains sticky without it)

Mix everything together in a saucepan over a medium heat until the dough reaches the right consistency (firm, but stretchy); turn out and knead for a few minutes.

Other table (or floor) activities should include a supply of paper and crayons or pencils. For this age group the thicker varieties of both are best—much less inclined to break, and they last much longer. However, anyone buying thick pencils needs to invest in a double-size sharpener at the same time unless they're a dab hand at sharpening with a vegetable knife. Hand-control is an important skill for a child to acquire, and he can never start wielding crayons and pencils too soon. If he appears to be losing interest in his scribbles, try directing him a little: can he copy a circle? how about a straight line? a zigzag? can he draw a kiss (a cross)? can he draw a big man, or a little man? can the man have some legs? how many? (Ooooh! he's a caterpillar!) Encourage the child to tell you about his pictures, and think of something complimentary to say about them. Failing all else, congratulating him on the colour ('That's a lovely yellow picture') or the size ('What a great big scribble you've made!') will be perfectly acceptable to the artist.

Felt pens for pre-schoolers serve no useful purpose; apart from making a mess, they don't actually help a child to learn to control a pencil, which is what he'll start off with at school.

While it is easy to make a mark with a felt pen, children who start off with them can find the transition to pencils frustrating because they have to learn afresh about the right pressure to use. A felt pen can be pressed quite firmly into the paper without any adverse effect; with a pencil, the same treatment will either break the lead or make a hole in the paper. With a pencil, a child can learn to use different pressures to gain different effects, whereas no such control is possible with a felt pen.

My second gripe concerning felt pens is that it is easy for a child to inadvertently leave off or lose the caps, causing colours to bleed wherever they are left, into clothes, covers or books, or to dry out, becoming hard and useless. In a perfect world all pens and pencils would be carefully tidied away after each use, but as most of us fall short of such an ideal, I believe that felt pens should be regarded as 'special' things that a child can look forward to using when he is old enough to appreciate and look after them.

Scissors are fascinating but frustrating things for young children. Most will persevere with them, though, because if they try often enough sooner or later they will achieve that satisfying crunch of cut paper, even if it's more by accident than design. Some of the flashy plastic ones designed for children are actually quite difficult to cut with, unless you have fairly stiff paper. In my experience, the best children's scissors are the old-fashioned round-ended metal ones such as most of us probably used in school and are still stocked by the Early Learning Centre today. Children who are not given the opportunity to use scissors before they go to school will experience a similar degree of difficulty in handling them at the age of five as they would have done at three, with the compounding embarrassment that most of their peers can already use them successfully. Once a child is fairly competent, scissors can be a source of endless inspiration, suitable for anything from cutting string or Sellotape to making 'snowflakes' or strings of paper people, cutting out pictures and model-making.

Jigsaws can hold a fascination for some children, and for almost all a great sense of achievement can be gained from putting together the first simple three- and four-piece puzzles. If the number of pieces attempted is built up gradually, a child who really enjoys this activity can often manage twenty-four- and thirty-piece puzzles before his third birthday. And you don't have to be continually buying new ones, since most children love the familiar and are perfectly happy to do a favourite puzzle over and over again. An inexpensive source of such concentrated entertainment (amongst other things) is the good old car boot sale.

Outdoor pleasures for this age group are accessible to most, and many of them are free. Visiting the local park, particularly in summer when you can take a picnic, can provide a whole day's fun. As well as swings and slides, there may be the added bonus of a shallow pool or sand-pit. The park is a great place to take a ball; there is space to throw or kick it, or a child can simply follow it where it rolls. He can play catch, bat it with an old racquet or stick, or enjoy any number of variations on that theme, without worrying about breaking windows or losing the ball over the garden fence. In autumn, many parks boast magnificent horse chestnut trees loaded with polished mahogany conkers; what joy to hunt for these treasures as they fall, and feel the soft felt inside their abandoned cases. Oaks, sweet chestnuts and pine trees too offer 'collectibles' that are fascinating to children. Trekking off with a plastic bag to the nearest horse chestnut tree may seem like foolishness to some adults, but for a young child the joy of filling it with as many conkers as can be found is a pleasure that defies rational explanation.

Most people have a park of some description within walking distance, but sometimes it can be more exciting for a little child to visit somewhere far enough away to necessitate the

use of a bus. For children who normally walk, or who travel
everywhere by car, the promise of a bus ride is really something to look forward to. A walk in the country can be an
education too, for parents and children alike. Little people who
are usually buggy-bound discover there the freedom to run,
hide and climb to their heart's content in ways not possible
in the city. Any such trip could usefully be undertaken with
the addition to the family picnic of some stale bread, for tearing
into small pieces and throwing to any appreciative ducks that
might cross your path. The fun of fresh-air activities can be
compromised by the bumps and grazes that some children
manage so successfully to collect; another damper can be the
ever-present horror of dog mess, particularly in city parks. The
best remedy for either of these is a supply of tissues and baby
wipes on any such outing and the foresight—like that of a
good boy scout—to be prepared.

Most children, even those who firmly believe that legs were
made for sitting in cars, will enjoy a walk on a sparkly autumn
day if they know they'll be able to scrunch through the fallen
leaves on the way and pick up some favourites to take home.
And what a way this can be to teach an appreciation of colours!
On a rainy day, if the child is equipped with wellies and
waterproofs, even a walk round the block can satisfy a passion
for puddles that little else can rival.

Back at home a paddling-pool in the garden in summer will
provide as much pleasure as, if not more than, a trip to the
baths, especially if another child is invited to share the fun.
Some children find public swimming pools quite intimidating,
not only because of the amount and depth of water but also
because of the noise. A paddling-pool has provided countless
hours of fun for my children and their friends, and is one piece
of equipment I would not be without, even though it is used
for less than half the year. Of course, such young children
must be constantly supervised whenever a paddling pool is in
use. I often had to cry 'Everybody out!' if the phone rang or

A passion for puddles.

when one little person needed the loo. However, there are plenty of water activities which the children can enjoy without getting into the pool (even fully clothed). These can often be safely supervised from a room overlooking the garden, perhaps while you're ironing or peeling the spuds if your kitchen window overlooks the paddling pool.

Our pool has been used for all sorts of fun: home-made paper boat races (blowing them across the pool before they sank); bathing dollies; 'finding out' what floats and what doesn't; filling up water pistols (usually empty squeezy bottles); bouncing balls into the water—the idea being to create as much spray as possible; pouring and measuring activities (how many cups of water will fill the bucket?); and watering the plants at the end of the day. New interest could be created by the addition of a little food colouring to dye the water, or bubbles (washing-up liquid!) to make it more exciting.

Another simple pleasure which most children enjoy is blowing bubbles. And when the first solution is used up it's quick, cheap and easy to make your own from one part washing-up liquid to two parts water, depending on the strength of your detergent.

Rhyme, rhythm and rap

Children can learn through the use of rhythm all sorts of things that it would be very difficult to teach 'straight'. My youngest daughter, who was the least gifted of the three at conversation, learnt to say the alphabet before her third birthday by repeating rhythmically three- and four-letter sequences. I would say them; she would repeat the sound *and* the rhythm, and I would then continue with the next short sequence. Sometimes I would sing the letters, which she would again copy: letters, rhythm and tune. This uses the same principle as many marching songs, in which the first voice is echoed by the second. We would use this very effective technique when we were walking to or from school or the shops.

Before they ever say it, many children learn the alphabet by singing it. This is a favoured method in 'Sesame Street', and one reason why the programme is so valuable. Suitable tunes that fit or that can easily be adapted to the alphabet include 'Little brown jug', 'Twinkle, twinkle, little star', 'Mary had a little lamb' and 'Humpty Dumpty', to name a few. As well as nursery rhymes, finger rhymes and poems, some children take great delight in learning tongue-twisters; my first daughter amazed us all by learning 'Peter Piper picked a peck of pickled pepper' at the age of two, largely through hearing it on a nursery tape, and when she was eight she could say the 'red lorry, yellow lorry' twister better than her mother. (Try it!)

My middle daughter at the same age loved the 'tickle tiger' poem:

> '*Stop* it!' cried the tiger,
> 'I'm ticklish, can't you see?
> I'm ticklish on my stripes,
> I'm ticklish on my knee!'
> '*Stop* it!' cried the tiger,

'There's something I must do.
It's time for *me* to tickle—
For *me* to tickle *you*!'

Often children are restricted more by *our* lack of imagination and effort than by any lack of ability or interest on their part. It is worth remembering that they can learn a great deal through fun.

8   From Three and a Half to Five

Be positive

One of the most important teaching strategies—and this applies to all children—is to give positive instructions rather than negative ones. 'Jump over the puddle!', for instance, is much more likely to achieve the required reaction than 'Don't step in that puddle!' It is so easy to say 'Don't', but much more effective to say 'Do'. Children are no different from the rest of us in that they dislike being told what they *can't* do, especially when it's something that they'd actually quite like to do! An instinctive reaction to 'Don't' is 'Why not? I want to!' It is much easier for a child to respond positively to positive instructions than negative ones. Similarly, 'Don't sniff' is better replaced by 'Stop sniffing, find a tissue and blow your nose!' Too many 'Don'ts' sound like nagging, and little people don't like to be nagged any more than big people do.

When children respond positively to our instructions, their obedience should be noticed and acknowledged, not with sweets, treats or money, but with a smile or a hug or a plain but heartfelt 'Thank you!', if that is appropriate. Appreciation from someone they love is a great motivator for a child.

If one child is 'showing off' and being silly, and another is behaving well, it will often be more effective to give positive attention to the latter rather than show disapproval to the child who is behaving badly. For example:

'Isn't Tommy sitting up nicely?! What a clever chap!'

or

'Rebekah *is* trying hard with her knife and fork—well done!'

This won't work in every situation, but it's always worth a try. Do make sure, though, that praising good behaviour doesn't result in letting the other child get away with his naughtiness—for instance, not tidying up his share of the toys.

Time out

There are two types of behaviour that children must not be permitted to get away with: deliberate, repeated defiance, and spitefulness (intentionally hurting another child). In either of these cases it would be appropriate to respond with 'time out' or a smack, first as an immediate punishment for such naughtiness, and second as a deterrent to the child's repeating the behaviour.

'Time out' simply means removing the child from the situation for a set period, or until he is ready to say sorry. The length of the time out depends on the age and understanding of the child, and possibly also on the nature of the 'offence', and the place for the time out to be spent will vary likewise. When my children were little we acquired a 'naughty chair'. Here the child would sit—and usually sulk—until she was released from her purgatory. Before freedom was granted, she was expected to apologise for the behaviour that had sent her there, and she always did—partly because it was what she had been trained to do, and partly because she knew that the apology was her passport back into the mainstream of family activity. We also used a 'naughty stair' to the same effect. As the children became older the time-out punishment might take place in their bedrooms, particularly if they were in a temper. The understanding in this case was that they would come downstairs *when they were ready*, when they had calmed down, thought about it and wanted to say sorry. Sometimes even four- and five-year-olds need a little space, and this allows them to cool off in their own time. Some children will take longer than others, and this system allows them to decide for themselves rather than pressurising them to make a grudging and insincere apology before they are ready.

Time out does not have to be spent in a bedroom or some other place away from the mainstream of activity. Its main purpose is not to isolate or reject the child, but to demonstrate a non-acceptance of the attitude or action that he has just shown. This can take place just as effectively in the room in which the child misbehaved. The punishment aspect of time out is the combination of unmistakable disapproval with an immediate, if temporary, restraint on the child's activities. The length of time incurred need not be excessive: two minutes can be a long time for a three-year-old; ten minutes may be more appropriate for a four-year-old. Inevitably, for most parents there will be times when the child isn't the only one who needs to calm down! On these occasions time spent in another room can be more effective for all concerned, and may facilitate a longer cooling-off period, if that is what's needed. What is important at the end of the time out is that the child understands, through a cuddle or a few words or both, that *although his behaviour was naughty and should not be repeated, he himself is loved.* Time out should leave him with the knowledge that his behaviour was unacceptable, not that he himself has been rejected.

If a child refuses to stay in his time-out place, or leaves it before he has done his time, he should be firmly told to return to the 'naughty chair', or whatever, and warned that if he leaves again before he is told to, he will be smacked. For those parents who would rather not smack their children, time out can be very effective, but even this kind of behaviour management may sometimes need to be backed up with a smack, or the threat of one.

Bad behaviour should never be ignored. But if a child is tired or unwell, or has suffered a family trauma, then of course allowances should be made. Often, dealing with bad behaviour *justly* is not a simple matter of doling out some punishment or other. As mentioned earlier, naughtiness may be prompted by boredom, or a feeling of neglect (particularly if there is a new baby in the family), and it may be that it is the cause of the behaviour that needs to be addressed rather than the behaviour itself.

A new baby

When I was expecting our youngest child, my second daughter was four. Unlike her older sister who had always been very independent, wanting to be a 'big girl' almost before she was a little girl, Bekah had always been content in her role as 'Mummy's baby'. One bedtime shortly before the birth, when we were all talking about the expected arrival, without thinking my husband said to her, 'You won't be Mummy's baby much longer, Bekah!' Well, she didn't say anything, but the look on her face told all: it was as though her whole world had collapsed. She was just crushed. Fortunately, inspiration struck, and I told her that she could be my 'big baby' for as long as she wanted, and the baby in Mummy's tummy would be our 'little baby'. Those few hasty but carefully chosen words reassured her completely that she would not be displaced by the newcomer, and we had no problems after that. But it could have been very different.

Both before and after the birth we deliberately referred to the expected child as '*our* baby', not 'Mummy's baby' or even 'the baby', and I believe that helped too. It gave both of the older girls a feeling of being special: other children might have special toys, but *they* had a new baby, and that was the most special of all. We were also very fortunate in that many friends who came with a gift for the new baby also brought small gifts for Abbey and Bekah, and most made a point of talking to them about their new sister *before* making a fuss of Bethany. In fact, they were both quite disappointed when the providential flow of well-wishers abated, because it meant that their unseasonable supply of gifts dried up too!

If a child's bad behaviour is born of boredom, as opposed to jealousy or lack of attention, the answer may be to provide him with something more interesting to do. The best way to un-bore a bored child over three years of age is not to buy him a new video, but to provide him with a supply of paper, pencils (not felt pens) and scissors, topped up with any or all of the following: glue, Sellotape, string, paint, old birthday cards, empty boxes, yoghurt pots, cotton wool—and, best of all, a friend to work with! Provided the mess is kept in one place (the table?), it won't be too difficult to clear up and, with a modicum of input from you or another adult, these things will provide hours of stimulating and absorbing play. The required input might be as simple as suggesting the child make and decorate a hat or crown, or a paper dress for dolly, or a mask to surprise Daddy with! Children who are given the opportunity to be creative in this way often know exactly what they need, and are quite able to specify what they want—they won't need *all* the raw materials every time. It's a good idea to make them ask for things like glue and Sellotape as and when they need them, and sometimes to make do without the Sellotape (unless you own shares in the stuff). There are so many things that can be used for this sort of activity, and it's handy to have a 'useful box' or 'black hole' to put suitable items in as they become available.

Be *quiet*!

Noise, and ever-increasing volume, can be one of the most stress-inducing factors associated with young (and not so young) children. But it doesn't have to be. Dealing effectively with noise is partly a matter of technique and partly a matter of training. The *technique* is for the parent, and the *training* is for the child!

Children do not need to shout and scream in order to have a good time—but they will if you let them. If an activity or game becomes too noisy, *change* it, or confiscate the source of the noise after an appropriate warning. If you cannot make yourself heard over the din, make a sudden and very loud noise—blow a whistle, thump the table, bash two saucepan lids together, drop one on the floor!—to get their attention. Then, in a carefully controlled, no-nonsense voice tell them to play more quietly, and *warn* them that they will have to do something different if they don't play properly. If one child ignores the warning, remove him from the source of the noise (and fun!) and give him something specific (and quiet) to do until he has shown that he can behave. A puzzle or book, or a piece of paper to draw on, will usually calm him down. Sometimes it may be more effective, having got the children's attention, to then drop your voice to a whisper, and tell them that they too must whisper for the next ten minutes—until you can hear yourself think again! Or tell them you want them to be quiet enough for it to be possible to hear a pin drop, and have a pin handy to drop. Making a game of it can work just as well as a more authoritarian approach and can achieve the same result: calmer, quieter children. Variety is the spice of life!

If children are making too much noise in the garden, first catch one of them. The others will soon run up to find out what it's all about. Don't fall into the trap of screaming 'Stop that noise!' from the window. Children need to understand that other people have a right to enjoy their gardens in relative peace and quiet. Most don't object to childish chatter and laughter—in fact, many rather enjoy it. But there's a big difference between that and the uncontained noise that can make neighbours' lives a misery. The irony is that children who are

Don't fall into the trap of screaming, 'Stop that noise!' from the window.

not constrained in the amount of noise they create often do not play as happily as those who are more controlled; they end up shouting *at* each other instead of *to* each other, and tears and skirmishes often result.

If a child is doing, or about to do, something either naughty or potentially dangerous, shout out his name—to get his attention—followed by a very clear instruction: 'Stop that!', 'Come here!' But then wait until the child has reached you, or you have reached him, before continuing in a suitably no-nonsense voice. Develop the habit of addressing a child *by name* when giving any instructions. Otherwise, when he is not the only child present, he will usually convince himself that you were speaking to the other one. In a group situation the instruction, 'Matthew, please put that in the bin', will be much more satisfactory than 'Somebody please put that in the bin.'

Shouting is very much like smacking, in that it can be extremely effective providing it is not over-used. There is a not so subtle distinction between shouting *to* a child and shouting *at* him. Bellowing his name in order to get his attention, or to relieve the parental frustration caused by the discovery that he's left the tap running *again*, is entirely different from screaming at him about it for the ensuing half-hour. People who unthinkingly shout at their children when they are small will find that as the child gets older they will have to shout louder and longer to achieve the same effect and sooner or later the child will copy the example he has learnt and begin shouting back. Habitual shouting by a parent usually denotes a lack of patience and may indicate frequent, if temporary, loss of self-control. It is important to recognise that shouting can often be classified as verbal bullying, with all the intimidation and inadequacy that that implies. As mentioned earlier, words used the wrong way can have a devastating effect on self-image. Any parent who becomes aware that she is reacting too often in this way needs to try to sort out her own problems before they cause greater difficulties for her child.

Shouting is a stressful habit to get into, anyway, and usually indicates a loss of control on the part of the shouter. Speaking as one who has a fairly short fuse, it is a lot easier to control the volume in the first place than control the words that will burst out if that control is lost. Clenching your jaw and slowly counting to ten is often a surprisingly effective safeguard against the flood of hurtful things that would only make a tense situation worse, and that you would regret the instant they'd left your lips. Neither parental authority, nor children's obedience, is determined by how loud we can shout.

A natural reaction for most children is to holler 'Mum!' the minute they can't find something. And some think nothing of yelling for their mother with no greater reason than suddenly wanting to know what's for tea. This sort of 'Come hither, slave, you *are* my mum after all' attitude has never gone down too well in our house—the management doesn't like it! It's worth persevering with the idea that your child's legs and eyes are more effective at finding the person, object or information of his desire than his lungs alone. Encourage your child to come and find you when he wants you, rather than just scream

'Mum'. Also, emphasise that there is a difference between *calling* and *shouting*, and that when a call goes unanswered it's time to activate the legs. This is equally true when the boot is on the other foot. Shouting for a child when calling to him has produced no response is always a trigger for tempers to start ticking, and the child who may have been genuinely lost in a world of make-believe gets treated to the same parental haranguing as the child who has simply turned up the selective-deafness knob. The best way round this is to train your child to always acknowledge when he has heard you, by responding 'OK', 'Coming' or whatever, and if he doesn't—and only then—to go and investigate.

Language and limits

With pre-schoolers, a very common conflict situation occurs when a child asks a question but doesn't get the answer he hopes for. If 'Can I have some sweets, Mummy?' elicits the 'No' response, he asks the question again—and again and again—in the hope that the answer will change. Resist giving in. Otherwise, he will learn that if he pesters you long enough he'll get what he wants in the end. When that has proved successful the first time, he'll know what to do the next time, and the time after that. Rather, when he asks you the second time, repeat your answer and then say:

1 'Did you hear me?'   (Get his answer.)
2 'What did I say?'   (Get his answer.)
3 'Do you understand?'   (Get his answer.)

Making a child confront the fact that he has heard you some-how helps him to accept what you have said, and may help avoid a tantrum. Sometimes it's polite to add a sweetener to your answer: for instance,

'You can have some sweeties *after dinner* if you eat it all up. OK?' (Get his response!)

or

'We can't go to the park today, but we'll go *tomorrow* if the sun shines.'

Try to soften negative responses with something positive to look forward to on another occasion.

The exasperated parent who finally gives in to the child who has worked himself into a tantrum is positively reinforcing that bad behaviour. The child who begins a strop every time he hears the word 'No' is undoubtedly one whose parents have continually given in to his 'bullying' and immaturity. If he has previously learnt that he can get his own way through a specific behaviour mechanism (a tantrum), he will be unable to balance that experience with the knowledge or understanding that what he wants—as opposed to what he needs—may be unhelpful or even bad for him. Such reinforcement of poor behaviour may well influence his developing ability to 'reason', and will certainly frustrate and inhibit his growing need and desire to act sensibly and thus gain praise and positive attention from good behaviour.

The experience that he has the 'power' to shift or demolish boundaries will be likely to produce a child who, although desperate for firm limits, will be unable to trust those he is given unless he pushes them and they remain unmoved. Any child in such a situation is likely to feel insecure because his abiding impression is that rules are relative to his rages.

Children have to—need to—accept that there are times when 'No' means 'No' without compromise, when opposition is fruitless. Defiance when a parent has said 'no' should never be rewarded by the spectacle of her having been ground into defeat. This does far more harm than just making it more difficult to say and mean 'no' on another occasion: it also upsets the whole balance of the relationship between parent and child. Children need their parents to be in control, to have the final word. This is part of the process of inculcating respect.

While children's vocabulary and understanding increase by leaps and bounds, their grasp of grammar and tense usually makes less than spectacular progress. This is completely normal and no cause for concern. If a child is hearing the correct words from the adults around him, he will eventually pick up that mode of speech. Correcting a wrong word or tense will help him learn more quickly, but only if it is done in an unobtrusive way. When a wrong word is used—'We singed', 'I brang/brung'—never repeat the incorrect word, but say the correct version ('You sang, did you?', 'You brought it, did you?'. The child will probably repeat your correction, but don't worry if he doesn't, it's *hearing* it that's important. Similarly, if he uses a word that is inappropriate, without putting too much emphasis on the 'bad' word offer him a substitute.

Sometimes it isn't just individual words that children get wrong, but whole phrases. When I was teaching in a south London primary school, the most common playground request was 'Can I go a loo, Miss?' Told to ask properly, many had no idea of how to phrase the question, and would hop from one leg to the other until they desperately intoned after me, 'Please may I go to the toilet?'

Speaking correctly is important; children who are unaware of their incorrect use of spoken English will be the more handicapped when they go to school and have to write it.

Teaching your child

Children of nursery age (three and a half plus) really can soak up information as sponges do water. But we have to provide the water! A child in an experientially sterile home will no more absorb knowledge than he will be stimulated. Children of this age can understand and remember far more than many adults realise, and while they may live up to *our expectations* as far as their intellectual capacities are concerned, this is not the same as reaching anything like *their potential*.

Practicalities

All children of nursery age should at least know their own name! Some start at nursery having never been called by the name written on the school register. Having a pet name for a child is fine, provided that he is also familiar with the name on his birth certificate, or that the school is informed of the name he is used to. The staff at one nursery suspected that a certain child was profoundly deaf because he never responded to his name. When this concern was mentioned to his parents, all was revealed: what they actually called him was not Carl but 'Bubba'. *Bubba*! And he wasn't even the youngest in his family.

It is also useful for a child to know his surname and be able to say it clearly, particularly in classes where there may be two or three or more children sharing the same first name. Learning their address and being able to say it clearly is something many children don't do, not because they can't, but because it has never occurred to their parents to teach it. Knowing what to do if they ever get lost is vitally important to teach at this age, as is the 'Don't talk to strangers' message. We don't need to frighten our children, but we do need to prepare them a little for the world out there.

Most children are fascinated by telephones, and usually enjoy talking on them even if it is only to say hello. Teaching them their telephone number may not seem necessary if they know their address, but why not teach it anyway? It's all good memory practice and they'll have to learn it sooner or later. Rhythm can transform learning by rote from something utterly boring to something that is fun and easy. Jazz up your telephone number with a rhythm in your voice and a finger click or a toe tap—move over, Fred Astaire!—and see how your child will *want* to copy that rhythm *and* remember the numbers almost incidentally. Learning can be so much fun for the child, as can teaching for the adult. And what a great sense of pride and achievement for both when the three-year-old correctly recites his address and phone number, and then asks to learn 'Granny's number too'.

The use of rhythm also taught my children the spelling of their names before they could actually write them. Rebekah's name was misspelt one day on pictures she'd created at nursery. Although she couldn't yet write her name unaided herself she knew what it looked like, and so she was able to remind the helper how to spell it when she saw that it was wrong.

Numbers

The learning processes involved with understanding numbers can be divided into four distinct stages:

1 the ability to repeat numbers in the right order (1–10 at this age);
2 the ability to count a limited number of objects;
3 the ability to select a specified number of objects from a greater number, thus demonstrating a practical understanding;
4 the ability to recognise, and name, written numbers.

If children are used to hearing numbers, not only in songs, rhymes and books but also from practical experience of counting buttons, stairs and so on, they will be familiar with the names of those numbers and the order in which they come. Memorising numbers up to ten should not pose a challenge or feat of memory too taxing for the average three-year-old.

Being able to count correctly a group of objects is a more complicated procedure, but still well within the capabilities of most pre-school children. When you study a number book with your child, count slowly and use your finger to point to each picture or object, starting at the top left of the page and moving across and down as you would read or write. If the number is printed on the page, trace it with your finger (always starting from the top) as you tell your child, or ask him, what it is. When you have counted the rabbits that match '3', ask him to count them too. If he loses interest, let him find another picture he likes better—or put the book away if he's had enough. Never coerce a child into continuing if he doesn't want to; learning at this age should be fun, not forced labour.

Being able to select a requested number of objects demonstrates that a child is developing an understanding of numbers. The simplest techniques will help him learn, remember and understand basic number concepts. Start off with numbers 1 and 2, and slowly extend the range as he becomes confident with each new digit. All my children have enjoyed playing with pegs—helping to hang out the washing was usually a favourite activity; I would ask them for one, two or three pegs, sometimes specifying the colour, and they would do their best to oblige. It would have been much faster to do it unaided, but speed and efficiency were not the point of the exercise. Children do like 'helping', and there are all sorts of little tasks they can enjoy but also learn from: for instance, setting the table, which involves choosing the right number of place-mats, spoons, forks; bringing a requested number of apples or onions to the cook, and so on.

A simple game that can be played anywhere is 'Show me'. 'Show me one finger, three fingers, five fingers, ten!' Wait until the child is confident with one hand before moving on to two. You might vary this activity by asking him to count *your* fingers, and then show the same number of fingers on his own hand. Very young children will need help with the physical aspect of curling some fingers down while leaving others upright. Use the thumb to hold the little finger down when it is not required.

When the child can do this confidently, start him off on simple addition using his fingers to count on. Fingers were made long before beads, blocks or other 'counters', and have the additional advantages of not dropping on the floor, getting lost or causing squabbles! Begin with numbers lower than six, so that he can use one hand for each number he is given. If you ask 'What does three plus two make?', help him to find three fingers on one hand and two on the other before putting both hands together and counting the total. Show him first using *your* fingers; invite him to ask you to do a 'sum' but get him to check your answer—you might have got it wrong! When these small numbers become too easy introduce larger ones, still keeping the total under eleven, until he is confident with this new stage. Children will often develop their own strategies for coping with larger numbers: one of mine started to use her nose as an additional counter when she ran out of fingers, and then tapped out on her chin the larger number before using her fingers to illustrate and count out the second number!

Numbers can be a source of great pleasure to many children. As they become competent at each stage, most will demand something harder to do and proceed to tackle it with enthusiasm.

The ability to recognise a printed squiggle as a shape representing a certain number can be nurtured with the use of simple 'flash cards'. On one side write the number and on the other draw the equivalent number of dots in a line. These are self-checking cards—if the child isn't sure if he has got the number right, he can find out for himself by counting the dots on the back. If you have more than one child of a similar age they can play with these together, testing (and checking) each other. Start with numbers 1, 2, 3, 4, 5 before progressing to 6, 7, 8, 9, 10 and beyond, if appropriate.

Once the child has reached this stage, he will probably want to start writing the numbers down; the only 'rule' to remember is to start from the *top* of each figure with the exception of number 5, when it is best to start with the 'down' line, adding the horizontal stroke last. Children who begin with the horizontal line often find that their number 5 resembles an 'S' shape, and they then have difficulty restoring the 90° angles of the correctly written number. It may help to make up 'stories' for some numbers—number 6: 'Down the slide and round the roundabout'; number 5: 'A little man with a big, fat tummy and last of all a cap on his head'. Don't be concerned if a number is written the wrong way round—this is very common, and will recur many times with some children before the penny finally drops. When it happens, make a joke of it: 'Naughty number three, he's back to front *again!*' When my children were practising numbers, they would have several goes at copying a certain number, and then we would decide which was the best one and draw by it a 'smiley' face.

One little girl I used to childmind for a couple of hours after her nursery class would beg and beg either to read or to do 'big girl sums', like her friends at 'big school', and would happily complete a whole page of simple addition before writing some sums herself for a dolly to do. She learned so quickly that before long she was also doing basic subtraction. The one-to-one attention that can be given to a child the year or so before he starts school, when he can be strongly motivated by praise and yet still want the intimacy and security of having a close adult involved and interested in what he is doing, constitutes an unbeatable and unrepeatable opportunity to stimulate and nurture his learning and his desire to achieve. Small children have a great sense of legitimate pride in their successes, and this should be encouraged; it not only spurs on further achievement and a joy in learning, but it also inculcates in the child a healthy confidence and a vital measure of self-esteem.

Teaching children to recognise the number patterns on a dice will open up many new games to them, including that old favourite, snakes and ladders.

Children who really enjoy the counting aspect of numbers, even as pre-schoolers, may drive you almost round the bend in their persistent attempts to count to a hundred. For some reason it's often a case not only of 'Mummy, listen' but also of the far more restricting 'Mummy, *watch* me, I'm counting'! When it all gets too much, try teaching them 'One, two, miss a few, ninety-nine, a hundred!'

Writing

One of the most important aspects of writing is starting off with the correct pencil hold. The pencil should be supported on the pad of the thumb, resting on the side of the middle finger and guided by the index finger. The Early Learning Centre stocks a simple device that will help correct a poor pencil hold.

The first word most children write is their own name. When you write it for them, begin with a capital and write the rest in small letters. Lower-case letters are more interesting and easier to distinguish than upper-case, which are all of the same height. It's an old-fashioned but nevertheless sound idea to draw a line for the child to write on, to encourage him to sit the letters neatly on it and to give a clear definition to those parts that extend below the line.

Show him how you write each letter, and encourage him to do the same. Most children can't copy from a model immediately, but they can trace over one. Use a yellow felt pen to write the name model, and then let him write over it in pencil. The felt pen will hardly show, and he will have produced his name in well formed if slightly wobbly letters. When he is familiar with the way individual letters are formed and has practised them by tracing over the model, get him to copy underneath it (draw him a line to write on). The final stage is practising without a model: now the child knows not only how to form the letters, but also how to spell his name. Some children will not be content with writing their name, but will want to add a description to every picture they draw. Encourage them to tell you what they want to say, then write down their words for them to trace or copy. Read the words out to them when they have finished, and then help them to read the sentence back to you.

Reading

Many children are ready and willing to start reading, or at least pre-reading activities, from the age of three and a half. Many parents, however, lack the confidence to begin to teach them and so the children miss out. Some parents seem afraid to do anything remotely educational with their offspring, preferring to leave it to the 'experts' when the children reach school age. But those who can already read when they start school have a big advantage, not only with reading itself but also in the confidence that the ability brings. This head start is usually maintained throughout the school career, and can be a predictor of future academic achievement.

Pre-reading activities begin with inculcating a familiarity with and an enjoyment of stories and books—something all children should experience from toddlerhood if not before. I believe it is also important for children to see adults enjoying their own books, not only the story-books that they read to *them*. The subliminal message that children receive should help them to think of books as fun, worthwhile and absorbing, fostering within them a desire to read themselves.

Learning the alphabet and becoming familiar with the names, sounds and appearance of letters are a crucial part of learning to read. There are many methods of teaching reading, and some are much more effective than others.

Those that do not concentrate on the basics of phonics (building up the individual letter sounds into words) are more frustrating and less rewarding than those based on a phonic approach. Teaching the alphabet is a good foundation for phonic work, and is so easily done. Follow this up on an *ad hoc* basis whenever the child looks at a picture dictionary: he can learn that the letter 'A', for instance, says 'a' as in 'apple' or 'ant', while you point out that the same letter occurs—twice—in his own name, Adam.

Try phonetic word games: thinking of words beginning with the same sound as the initial letter of his name is a simple start. When I used to walk to nursery with two three-year-olds we would sometimes play 'I can think of a word beginning with . . .', and we would try to find as many words as we could beginning with that letter sound. The person providing the last word would have the privilege of choosing the next letter. It takes some children longer than others to attune their ears to letter sounds in this way, and early on it's better to concentrate on one sound than to attempt several.

'I spy' is a good game to play *phonetically* when the child's ability to separate out the initial sound of a word is more firmly established. Even so you may find yourself trounced by words like 'phone', which he will say begins with 'f', and by words with silent first letters such as 'knee' and 'knot', 'gnat' and 'gnome', which your child insists begin with 'n'. Concede defeat graciously and remember that, *phonetically*, he is correct. When a word begins with the sound 'c' (as in 'cat' and 'kitten'), he has no way of knowing whether that means C or K, but in the early stages it really doesn't matter. There is plenty of time to distinguish between a 'curly c' and a 'kicking k' later on. The time to correct the *spelling* of the 'spied' object is when the child is familiar with the name, sound and appearance of most letters and is able to play the game using the *name* of the initial letter of his chosen word rather than the sound. Then you can explain that some words are tricky and that, for example, the word 'phone' uses the letters 'p' and 'h' to make an 'f' sound, so that it actually begins with 'p'. You can then give further examples of 'ph' sounding like 'f'.

I taught my own children and those I childminded with a combination of flash-cards and phonetics. I began by teaching them to recognise their own names written on a small piece of card, and then added mummy, daddy and the names of siblings on similar cards. When they were confident with these names, I added 'house', 'garden', 'in' and 'the'. Teaching the children to recognise the initial letter sound of each word helped in their memorising of each word shape. 'The' was used to explain that not all words can be sounded out phonetically—some you just have to learn. Some of the children needed clues to help them remember the words. These could range from a letter 'story', such as pointing out that 'd' is tall like daddy; to a visual clue on the word itself, such as drawing some smoke coming from the 'chimney' of 'house'; to putting my tongue between my teeth to demonstrate the first sound in 'the'. Even with that small number of words, short phrases could be formed: 'Bekah/mummy/daddy in the house/garden'. Adding 'is' was an opportunity to make a sentence and also to teach the phonetic sounds of 's' and 'n' combined with 'i'. Being able to understand the phonetic make-up of a word is a big advance on simply memorising its shape. As the child learned a word, so a new one would be added to her word box (any receptacle used for storing the word cards); sometimes it would be my choice, sometimes hers.

Once the word box became established, I started my children off on a reading scheme. New words from the scheme were added to the word box and sounded out phonetically as appropriate. Each child had the opportunity to recognise and read the words both in and out of context.

Not all words can be sounded out in this way; 'the', 'there', 'that' and 'with' are clear examples of this. However, most children will quickly learn the sound that 'th' makes, particularly if you emphasise poking out the tongue in order to make it. Other common words that cannot be sounded out often involve a 'silent' letter, as in 'when', and letter blends such as in 'shop' (sh) and 'chop' (ch). We used to say that silent letters didn't say anything because they had 'gone to sleep'.

Letter blends we learned as they came up, using 'clues' like
a finger on lips for 'sh' and a puffing steam train impression
for 'ch'. When you come to the 'ow' blend in 'cow' and
'how', you can be really imaginative! Many words cannot be
fully sounded out because they contain a 'magic e'—as in
'bike' and 'same'—which changes the vowel *sound* to its
name.

When my children were sounding out new words, they
became quite familiar with my saying, 'If "a" (the sound of
the letter) doesn't work, try "A" (its name).' Other useful
rules to point out include that while the letter 'Y' at the beginning of a word makes a 'y' sound (as in 'you' and 'yell'), at
the end of a word it copies its friend 'E' (as in 'mummy' and
'jelly') or its chum 'I' (as in 'by' and 'cry'). Repeated letters
(as in 'keep', 'sell' and 'daddy') are sounded only once.

There are very few words that do not give some phonetic
clue to their identity. Understanding basic rules about how
letters work together is a great help in the teaching of reading,
and will make the task easier—and more fun—for both parent
and child.

Word cards were discarded when the child could read the
word without hesitation, and a new one would be added. I
used the two Ladybird Key Words schemes; both are valuable
for their simple repetitive approach, building slowly on what
has gone before. The children all preferred the more modern
of the two, the 'Read with Me' series. They appreciated the
cartoon-like illustrations and enjoyed the antics of the naughty
dog, Sam. The older-style 'Peter and Jane' series has more
repetition and is useful for extra practice. When you read with
beginners, it is often helpful if their eyes are guided across
the page by means of a finger moving under the words as they
read them—they can use their own finger, but in the early
stages it's often better if you use yours. Ladybird also publish
the excellent 'Read it Yourself' series, each story of which is
matched to a reading level from the main scheme. Not much

can top the excitement of a young child who has just read his first story-book himself! It's a lovely time to enjoy and share with a baby bookworm.

After levels 4 or 5, the Ladybird, Key Words books lost their appeal for my children; but the groundwork that they had provided, complemented with the emphasis on phonetics that I had supplied, meant that a sound basis for reading progress had been established. The children realised that there were lots of other books that they could read on their own or with a little help, and soon had their own favourites. One in particular was the 'Bangers and Mash' series (phonetically based on the antics of two naughty monkeys), which we discovered at our local library and which they later found at school.

Even the keenest young reader will have off-days when she won't want to read or go through her word cards. There's no need to force the issue—she'll regain her enthusiasm soon enough. The time to read together is also an opportunity to snuggle up on the settee: a special time when the child has the undiluted attention of the adult, a cosy, reassuring time when words and learning and progress can be enjoyed in a relaxed and intimate way.

For those parents who would prefer a more structured phonic approach to the teaching of reading, the 'First Steps' video by Mona McNee[1] is an excellent starting-point, provided you focus on the quality of the instruction rather than the quality of the video itself—Walt Disney it ain't!

Many children who begin school already able to read experience the frustration of being given starter books—that is to say, books that assume no reading ability at all—to take home in their reading bags. Give the teacher a little while to assess the reading level of your child, but if after a couple of weeks the situation remains unchanged make an appointment to see her, or send her a letter. A bright child who is bored or disillusioned with school can become just as disruptive as any other, and there is no excuse for him to be ignored or held back because he has already achieved more than was initially expected of him.

I believe that any parent who wants to, and who is prepared to invest the time and effort, can teach her child to read. It does require patience, imagination, enthusiasm and commitment, but that is recompensed in full by the joy of achievement when your child learns another new word or says, 'Can we do reading now, Mummy?'

9 Looking to the Future

Being part of a family means belonging to that special refuge where there is freedom to be ourselves, but a restraining balance of loyalty, responsibility and care; where the right to be forgiven and still loved even when we've got things horribly wrong is a condition of membership, and where the security of being needed and the fulfilment of being loved, as well as the gift of being able to love, constitute the glue that binds it all together. As adults we need the buttress of a family behind us to reassure us in times of doubt, support us during periods of stress and sadness, and share with us our joys, hopes and successes. Adults who do not have or who have given up such a family sometimes experience an underlying emptiness—a futility, even—that permeates their lives. If as adults we need the stability of supportive and loving families around us, how much more do our children need it.

The first five years contain the experiences that, more than any others, will mould a child's attitudes and aspirations for the rest of his life. The Jesuits used to say, 'Give me the child until he is seven, and I will show you the man'; many a mother would say, 'Give me a child until he is five, and I will show you the future.' Because by the time a child reaches five the patterns for behaviour have already been established and parental attitudes and responses have made their mark, teachers of reception classes can often predict which of their children are likely to do well and which are likely to go off the rails before they leave school. Of particular significance during this early period is the opportunity for a child to bond with at least one consistent figure, preferably his mother. According to the child psychologist John Bowlby, who studied the traumas suffered by child evacuees during the war, 'What is believed to be essential for mental health is that the infant and young child should experience a warm, intimate and continuous relationship with his mother (or permanent mother substitute) in which both find satisfaction and enjoyment.'[1]

The significance of a mother's role cannot be overemphasised, and any government concerned about the state of social decay would do well to place the parenting issue, as opposed to the childcare issue, at the top of the political agenda. Professors John and Elizabeth Newson of Nottingham University maintain that community care is a poor second to parental care: 'The best that community care can offer is impartiality . . . but a developing personality needs to know that to someone it matters more than any other children, that someone will go to unreasonable lengths for its sake.' There is increasing evidence that further provision of day care for young children is the answer neither to the needs of the infants and their mothers, nor indeed to the wider needs of society. Far better that the huge financial resources proposed for subsidising government-funded childcare be reallocated to enable the mothers who want to care for their children, full-time, at home, at least during the pre-school years, to do so.

Given that children who are well socialised at five are generally well socialised at fifteen, and that the best socialising influence is thought to be in most cases the child's mother— who, generally speaking, can be relied upon to love and care for her child better than anyone else—rather than encouraging women to leave their pre-school children in nurseries and playgroups and with childminders, it would surely be better to encourage them to look after their under-fives themselves. But this would require a reversal of the feminist position that women can and should 'have it all ways'—have families and careers (or nannies and nervous breakdowns?)—and a radical reappraisal of parental roles and responsibilities. Perhaps a true feminist agenda would accept and address the concerns of the majority—62 per cent[2]—of employed mothers of pre-school children, who would rather be at home with them than out at work. If we value the family as the best place to bring up children, and if we believe that the natural ability and inclination of mothers to nurture the very young are generally greater than those of fathers, then there must be a determined political and social will to raise the profile of motherhood and the status of 'home-makers'.

Enhancing the self-image and the *public image* of those women who choose to make parenting their first priority, and acknowledging the crucial importance of that role, both in the individual family and in society at large, is fundamental. Recognition that there is no more important work than bringing up the next generation is vital, and must be demonstrated in practical and fiscal support. The simple mechanism of transferring the non-earning mother's tax allowance to her husband, and exempting non-earning mothers from paying council tax, would make a significant difference to many families who currently cannot afford for the mother to remain unwaged. The recognition in the tax system that marriage is a more secure base for bringing up children than cohabitation would be a small but significant step in the right direction. It would emphasise that fathers, too, are vital for healthy family life, and ensure that responsible, working dads are not financially penalised for having made a commitment to wife and family.

In any discussion of parenting it would be foolish and irresponsible to ignore the increasing numbers of struggling or inadequate parents, particularly young mothers, and even more particularly, young single mothers. Most of those amongst them who might justifiably be described as bad parents are so not because they have chosen to be so, but because they have been poorly parented themselves and have little in the way of

practical and emotional resources or family support. Yet these
are often the very mothers who are at home all day with their
increasingly boisterous children, and with very little idea of
what to do with them. Rather than spending vast amounts of
money providing childcare for mothers who don't want it, how
much more profitable to use it to establish parenting resource
centres which could offer practical advice to those who so
desperately need it. Help for those seeking it must become a
priority for all our sakes.

Children who are uncontrollable at three and four will not
suddenly become well socialised when they start school, and
mothers who cannot cope with their pre-schoolers are unlikely
to develop parenting wisdom as their children reach primary
age. Such children are often understood to be 'difficult' before
they start school; once there, they tend to become 'problems'
for their classmates and teachers as well as for their parents.

Parenting courses recognised, supported and partly funded
by local authority social services and education departments,
but run by a coalition of professionals and volunteers, could
offer a way forward. Providing crèche and nursery facilities
for the duration of each session would generate an opportunity
for practical and realistic parenting education without the distraction of bored children, offering support and where necessary additional back-up to participants. It would be hoped
that the volunteers would be those of proven parenting skills,
drawn from the community, including members of local church
and other community groups, the retired, the long-term
unemployed and, of course, full-time mothers, the career
home-makers. Such provision would not only offer practical
support and training for those who need it, but after the teaching and discussion part of the session would also provide an
opportunity for the parents to interact and play with their
children under the eyes of the tutoring and nursery staff.
Parenting skills may be taught in a lecture hall but can only
be learnt, and practised, in the company of children. Local

schemes such as this would also begin to re-establish the sense of a caring community in which the wisdom, experience and compassion of older mothers are recognised and respected.

For those who want to be full-time mothers for their children but know that they cannot afford to do so, it may be worth considering registering as a childminder. Childminding enabled me to stay at home with my children while contributing financially, which was important to me personally as well as essential for us as a family. By the time tax, National Insurance, childminding and nursery fees had been deducted from my salary as a teacher, I wouldn't have been much better off financially than I was as a childminder. The unexpected bonus with childminding was that I discovered that it was fun for my children to have other little friends to play with, and it helped them to learn to share, take turns, and play imaginatively together. It also made weekends even more precious because it meant we were 'just us' again, and could relax a little after a hectic week. Childminding other people's children also saves the hassle of finding a good childminder yourself!

Being a good parent doesn't necessarily come naturally, and rarely comes easily. It is a vocation that has to be worked at, the same as any other. Good discipline—as opposed to no discipline or inconsistent discipline—doesn't just happen, either: it too needs to be worked at. Becoming a parent is the beginning of a learning process for both parent and child in which control and order, routine and organisation, are equally important for both. Happy, well disciplined children are generally the product of loving, well disciplined parents: parents who understand how important it is to say yes to their little ones but who also are willing to say no *and stick to it* when they believe it to be the more appropriate response. It is important to try to get it right from the beginning—a child who has been lovingly disciplined from babyhood will be much easier, and happier, to live with than a child who has been lovingly allowed to run wild!

For most people, confidence in parenting develops through the practical experience of having their own child. Often, the knowledge of what works in a certain situation comes only after the experience of what doesn't work! Given the will and inclination to love their child, the most important thing that parents can give to him is their time. The younger the child, the more time he needs; and the more time they give him, the more they will receive back in the years to come. Establish good intentions, habits and behaviour while your child is in his infancy, and the effort and commitment will be repaid a thousand times as he grows up. A loving relationship based on trust and time spent together, with clear boundaries set for behaviour, and an understanding that parenting is a learning process, is the best long-term investment any of us can ever make.

Notes

CHAPTER 2   PRINCIPLES FOR PARENTING
1 David Robinson, 'The Psychology of Smacking Children', *The Irish Psychologist*, Feb. 1994.
2 David T. Lykken, 1995, *The Antisocial Personalities*, Lawrence Erlbaum Associates.
3 L. N. Robins and D. A. Regier, 1991, *Psychiatric Disorders in America*, The Free Press.
4 Richard Lynn, 'The Psychology of Smacking Children', *The Irish Psychologist*, Nov. 1993.
5 David T. Lykken, *The Antisocial Personalities, op. cit.*
6 G. R. Patterson, B. DeBaryshe, and E. Ramsey, 'A developmental perspective on antisocial behaviour', *American Psychologist*, 44, 1989.

CHAPTER 3   GRASPING THE NETTLE: TO SMACK OR NOT TO SMACK
1 Peter Newell and Martin Rosenbaum, Taking Children Seriously: A proposal for a Children's Rights Commissioner. Calouste Gulbenkian Foundation.
2 K. E. Palmerus and S. W. Scarr, April 1995, How Swedish parents discipline young children: Cultural comparisons and individual differences. (Paper presented at the biennial meeting of the Society for Research and Child Development, Indianapolis, IN.)
3 Robert E. Larzelere, February 1996, A Review of the Outcomes of Parental Use of Nonabusive or Customary Physical Punishment. (Paper presented at a conference on the short and long term consequences of corporal punishment.)

CHAPTER 4   BITING THE BULLET: THE TRUTH ABOUT SMACKING
1 Children Act 1989, Part 1, section 2, para 9; section 3, para 1.
2 A conversation with a psychologist who had interviewed violent prisoners revealed that many did not resent the severe discipline they had received as children, when they perceived it to be justifiable on the grounds of their behaviour. Their own rage and violent behaviour they attributed to the random, erratic and inconsistent punishment they had suffered through no fault of their own.
3 H. R. Schaffer, 'The issue of parental corporal punishment', Discussion Paper 88, submitted to the Scottish Law Commission.
4 Richard J. Gelles and Ake W. Edfeldt, 'Violence Towards Children in the United States and Sweden', *Child Abuse and Neglect*, vol. 10, 1996.

5 Ake W. Edfeldt and Joan Durrant, 1994, 'The Swedish 1979 *Aga* Ban plus Fifteen'. Research paper.

6 Peter Newell, 1989, *Children are People Too: The Case Against Physical Punishment*, Bedford Square Press.

7 *Independent*, 10 June 1996, Sweden's Rules on Corporal Punishment Lead the Way.

8 Joan E. Durrant, 1994, 'The Abolition of Corporal Punishment in Canada: Parents' versus Children's Rights'. Research paper.

9 R. E. Larzelere, 1993, 'Does a reduction in ordinary parental spanking reduce child abuse rates?' 'Baumrind (1973) reported that permissive parents, who were the least likely to use spanking, were most likely to report "explosive attacks of rage in which they inflicted more pain or injury on the child than they had intended . . . Permissive parents apparently became violent because they felt that they could neither control the child's behaviour nor tolerate its effect upon themselves." So it could be that prohibiting all spanking eliminates the type of mild spanking that serves to maintain control before escalating into a coercive cycle of violence. Using a mild spanking as a backup for less aversive discipline responses subsequently makes those less aversive responses more effective by themselves, thereby avoiding the coercive cycle of violence further.'

10 R. E. Larzelere, S. A. Alibrando, M. Klein and W. R. Schumm, 'Relations to spanking and other parenting characteristics to self-esteem and perceived fairness of parental discipline', *Psychological Reports*, no. 64, 1989.

11 S. A. Alibrando, 'The effect of corporal punishment and contextual parental characteristics on rebelliousness, neuroticism and introversion'. Unpublished paper.

12 D. Baumrind, 'Response to "A review of the outcomes of parental use of nonabusive or customary physical punishment"'. Paper presented at the conference on the Long and Short Term Consequences of Corporal Punishment, Chicago, 16 February, 1996.

13 R. E. Larzelere and J. A. Merenda, 'The effectiveness of parental discipline for toddler misbehaviour at different levels of child distress', *Family Relations*, no. 43, October 1994.

14 R. E. Larzelere, W. N. Schneider, D. Trumbull and P. Pike, 'The Effectiveness of parental punishment vs. reasoning in delaying misbehaviour recurrences in toddlers'. Unpublished research paper.

CHAPTER 8   FROM THREE AND A HALF TO FIVE

1 Mona McNee, Reading Reform Foundation, 2 Keats Avenue, Whiston, Merseyside L35 2XR. (The Reading Reform Foundation is a pressure group campaigning for the re-introduction of systematic phonics teaching in schools.)

CHAPTER 9   LOOKING TO THE FUTURE

1 John Bowlby, psychologist, quoted in *Full-time Mothers*, Spring 1996.

2 Patricia Morgan, *Daily Mail*, 29 October 1996.

Index

abuse: *see* child abuse
alphabet learning 140
anti-smacking legislation 52
   in Sweden 41, 42, 60, 68–72
anti-smacking lobby 56–74
antisocial personality disorder 32–3
apologising
   adult to child 40, 49
   child to child 47
arguments/debates 39
   versus reasoning 46
arrogant behaviour 15
Association of Directors of Social
   Services 65, 67
Association of Metropolitan
   Authorities 67
attention-seeking behaviour 103,
   111

babies 17
   disciplining 87–8
   establishing routines 81–4
   hair-pulling by 26, 88
   impact on siblings 145–6
   nappy changing 88–9
   personal account 79–81
baby talk 112–13
Baumrind, Diana 73
bedtime
   baby routines 81–4
   shared bedrooms 84–5

   in summer 29
bed wetting 116–17
behavioural psychology 33
bonding 79–81, 166
books 118
   learning to read 162–3
Bowlby, John 166
boys/girls 32–3
bribes 129
British Association for Community
   Child Health 67
British Association of Social
   Workers 66, 67
bullying and bullies 26
   verbal bullying 149

changing your mind 122
child abuse 56, 60
   NSPCC report 68
   physical violence 57–8, 61
   sexual abuse 61
   smacking and 60–1
   in Sweden 69
childcare 166
   see also childminder
childhood memories 9–10
childishness 123
Childline 67
childminder registration 28, 52, 169
   court case 52–3
childminder survey 54–5

Children Act (1989) 52, 53
Children's Legal Centre 63
Children's Rights Development Unit 63
Children's Rights movement 41, 56
Children's Rights Office 63
child's eye view 126
Christensen, Anna 71
comforters/dummies 96–7
Commission on Children and Violence 68
common sense 36–40
compromise 24
conscience development 27
corporal punishment 35, 36
  banned in state schools 63
counting games 119
creative play 135–6, 146

Daycare Trust 66–7
Defence for Children International 65–6
defiance 39, 130, 143
diabetes 131
discipline (*definition*) 15–16
distraction techniques 93–4
domestic violence 60
'Don't Talk to Strangers' 153
DuBose Ravenel, Dr S. 58
dummies 96–7

Early Learning Centre 136, 158
eating rules 132–4
Ek, Simone 70
Enuresis Research and Information Centre 67
EPOCH (End Physical Punishment of Children) 56–73

fathers/father-figures 33, 167
  approval from 130–1
felt pens 135–6
feminist views 166–7

financial aspects 167
First Steps (video) 163
flash cards 156, 160–1
food 131–4

games: *see* play
garden toys 118
girls/boys 32–3

hair-pulling 26
hand-control development 135–6
Harrold-Claesson, Ruby 60, 71, 72
'helping' their parents 155
hoovering 98–9
horseplay 21

inconsistent discipline 27, 34, 38

jigsaw puzzles 137

Kids' Clubs Network 66

labelling theory 28
Ladybird Key Words scheme 162–3
language acquisition 86–7, 113–14
  baby talk 112–13
  speaking correctly 152
  word games 119, 160
Larzelere, Dr Robert E. 73
Leach, Dr Penelope 63
learning processes 152–64
leaving a favoured place 128–9
loving parenting 21, 169–70
  unconditional love 25
Lykken, David T. 32, 33

McNee, Mona 163
manners 114
mother's role 166–7
musical games 140–1

National Association of Nursery Nurses 66

National Childminding Association 53–4, 66
National Children's Bureau 63
naughty chair 28, 143
'naughty children' debate 28
  apparent naughtiness 123–6
neighbours 14
Newell, Peter 63
Newson, John and Elizabeth 166
nicknames/pet names 153
night-lights 85–6
noise 146–50
NSPCC 68
number learning 154–8
nursery rhymes 117–18, 140–1

outdoor activities 137–9
  noise control 147–8

paddling-pool 138–9
parenting courses 168–9
penalties 16, 38
  see also punishment
personality differences 30–2
pet names/nicknames 153
phone: *see* telephone/telephone
  calls
phonetics 159–63
physical affection 21
physical violence 57–8
play
  creative 135–6, 146
  game playing 12
  noise control 146–8
  playing with children 119–20
  snakes and ladders 157
play-dough 135
please/thank you 113–14, 127
potty-training 114–17
praise 142–3
priority setting 97–9
privilege withdrawal 16
punishment 16

age of child and 17–18, 38
  see also smacking

Rayner, Claire 63
reading skills 159–64
respect (inculcating) 151
reward systems 12
rhymes 117–18, 140–1
right and wrong 26–30
Runske, Katarina 71

Save the Children Fund 67
Schaffer, Prof H. R. 61
schools
  arrogant pupils 15
  bright children 163–4
  corporal punishment banned 63
  independent 35
scissors 136–7
self-centred child 13
self-discipline (parental) 20
Sesame Street 134, 140
sex differences in socialisation
  32–3
sexual abuse 61
shame, use of 19
sharing/taking turns 127–8
shouting 148–50
single mothers 167–8
sleeping routines
  babies 81–4
  shared bedrooms 84–5
  in summer 29
smacking 41–51
  1992 court case 52–3
  anti-smacking arguments 56–63
  appropriate 42–3
  'bad' smacking 48–9, 62–3
  by teachers 55
  inappropriate 43–5
  ineffective 48
  smacking methods 19, 45–7, 74
  time out and 144

smacking – *cont.*
  of toddler 91–3, 101, 105
  UN Convention position 36
  of wriggly baby 88–9
socialisation 30–4
STOPP (Society of Teachers
    Opposed to Physical
    Punishment) 63
storybooks 118
  learning to read 162–3
strangers 153
Sweden 41, 42, 60, 68–72
Swedish Family Campaign
    Foundation 71
Swedish Opinion Research Institute
    69
sweets/sweet tooth 97

tantrums: *see* temper tantrums
tax system 167
teachers 21, 55
  STOPP 63
teaching your child 152–64
telephone/telephone calls
  learning own number 153
  not interrupting 21–2
television 57, 134
  eating in front of 134
  Sesame Street 134, 140
telling-off: *see* verbal disapproval

temper tantrums 44–5, 103–10
  due to not smacking 50–1
  giving in to 151
  personal account 105–10
thank you/please 113–14,
    127
time out 143–5
  naughty chair 28, 143
toddlers 91–120
toilet training 114–17
  personal account 115–16
toys
  improvised 118–19
  jigsaw puzzles 137
trainer-pants 116
Trumball, Dr Dan 58

UN Convention on Rights of the
  Child 35–6

vacuuming 98–9
verbal disapproval 16
  age of child 18
  for babies 87–8
violence 57–8
  domestic 60

word cards 160–1, 163
word games 119, 160
writing skjills 158–9